Perspectives on Happiness

At the Interface/Probing the Boundaries

Founding Editor

Rob Fisher (*Interdisciplinarian, Oxford, UK*)

Advisory Board

Peter Bray (*Programme Leader for Counsellor Education, School of Counselling, Human Services and Social Work Education and Social Work, University of Auckland, New Zealand*)
Robert Butler (*Professor/Chair, Department of History, Elmhurst College, Illinois, USA*)
Ioana Cartarescu (*Independent Scholar, Bucharest, Romania*)
Seán Moran (*Waterford Institute of Technology, Ireland*)
Stephen Morris (*Author and Independent Scholar, New York, USA*)
John Parry (*Edward Brunet Professor of Law and Associate Dean of Faculty, Lewis & Clark Law School, Portland, Oregon, USA*)
Natalia Kaloh Vid (*Associate Professor, Department of Translation Studies, Faculty of Arts, University of Maribor, Slovenia*)

VOLUME 121

The titles published in this series are listed at *brill.com/aipb*

Perspectives on Happiness

Concepts, Conditions and Consequences

Edited by

Søren Harnow Klausen, Bryon Martin,
Mustafa Cihan Camci and Sarah A. Bushey

BRILL
RODOPI

LEIDEN | BOSTON

Cover illustration: Cover design by Amanda Cordell, Graphic Design, HSU.

The Library of Congress Cataloging-in-Publication Data is available online at http://catalog.loc.gov
LC record available at http://lccn.loc.gov/2019935276

Typeface for the Latin, Greek, and Cyrillic scripts: "Brill". See and download: brill.com/brill-typeface.

ISSN 1570-7113
ISBN 978-90-04-38291-6 (paperback)
ISBN 978-90-04-39579-4 (e-book)

Copyright 2019 by Koninklijke Brill NV, Leiden, The Netherlands.
Koninklijke Brill NV incorporates the imprints Brill, Brill Hes & De Graaf, Brill Nijhoff, Brill Rodopi, Brill Sense, Hotei Publishing, mentis Verlag, Verlag Ferdinand Schöningh and Wilhelm Fink Verlag.
All rights reserved. No part of this publication may be reproduced, translated, stored in a retrieval system, or transmitted in any form or by any means, electronic, mechanical, photocopying, recording or otherwise, without prior written permission from the publisher.
Authorization to photocopy items for internal or personal use is granted by Koninklijke Brill NV provided that the appropriate fees are paid directly to The Copyright Clearance Center, 222 Rosewood Drive, Suite 910, Danvers, MA 01923, USA. Fees are subject to change.

This book is printed on acid-free paper and produced in a sustainable manner.

Contents

Notes on Contributors   VII

Introduction   1
   Søren Harnow Klausen, Bryon Martin, Mustafa Cihan Camcı and Sarah A. Bushey

1 Happiness in the Routine of Everyday Life   7
   Mustafa Cihan Camcı

2 Against 'Feeling Good': Aristotle's Concept of Happiness (*eudaimonia*)   14
   A. Erdem Çifçi

3 Utility, Liberty, and the State's Duty to Promote Flourishing   20
   Andrew Molas

4 What Makes College Students Happy? A Day Reconstruction Study   29
   Ranjeeta Basu and Marie D. Thomas

5 Hegemonic Systems and the Politics of Happiness: the Fairy Tale as Ideology   41
   Sheila M. Rucki and Lisa Ortiz

6 Using Art Therapy Techniques to Explore Home Life Happiness   50
   Emily Corrigan-Kavanagh, Carolina Escobar-Tello and Kathy Pui Ying Lo

7 What Is the Good Life: an Overview of the 'Good Life' at the University of Florida   64
   Sarah A. Bushey

8 The Vocation Fulfilment: a Driver for Happiness at Work   72
   Andrea-Mariana Marian and Valeriu Budeanu

9 Classic Cars and Happiness: a Profile of Participants and Their Family, Community and Cultural Health   80
   Bryon Martin

10 Happiness and the Structure and Dynamics of Human Life   88
    Søren Harnow Klausen

11 Quo Vadis: Fullness or Emptiness in the Pursuit of Happiness?   98
    Robert D. Hermanson

12 Earthly Happiness and Heavenly Happiness   108
    Seán Moran

13 Happiness in Higher Education in Hong Kong: an Anthropology Study   117
    Kelly K. L. Chan

14 Re-Embracing Simplicity: an Exploration of Epicurean Happiness   129
    Julia Hotz

15 The Subjective Well-Being of Married Women In and Out of the Workforce in Sri Lanka   140
    Ann Shelomi Panditharatne

16 The Sublime Landscape   159
    Jane Russell-O'Connor

    Index   167

Notes on Contributors

Ranjeeta Basu
is Professor of Economics at California State University San Marcos. Her areas of expertise include Economics and Wellbeing, International Economics and Econometrics.

Valeriu Budeanu
is a senior consultant in finance and economics fields. During his career, he has been working in environments like banking systems, production companies, winding up companies, the Romanian Justice Department, penitentiaries administration, the United Nations (just to mention a few), where he had the opportunity to work with and to make observations on a wide range of employees and employers.

Sarah A. Bushey
is an adjunct instructor and Assistant Director of the course What is the Good Life at the University of Florida. She graduated in April 2015 with a doctorate in musicology and also holds degrees in music education and performance. In summer of 2018, she moved to her home town in Norther Maine and now owns and operates a bakery

Mustafa Cihan Camcı
is an Associate Professor in the department of Philosophy in Akdeniz University, Antalya, Turkey. He teaches phenomenology, particularly Heidegger, modern Turkish literature, philosophy of art and philosophy of identity.

Kelly K. L. Chan
is a second year PhD candidate in the School of Health and Education at Middlesex University London. Her current research focuses on happiness in higher education in Hong Kong. She examines happiness using visual ethnography.

A. Erdem Çifçi
is Associate Professor at the Department of Philosophy in Mersin University in Turkey. His main research interest is in phenomenology. He also has an interest in humanistic (existential) psychotheraphy.

Emily Corrigan-Kavanagh
is a Research Fellow in Communication Design from the University of Surrey. Her PhD research, undertaken at Loughborough University, looked at how design and creativity can be used to improve sustainability and happiness in the home, in particular, art therapy techniques within service design.

Carolina Escobar-Tello
is Lecturer in the Loughborough Design School at Loughborough University and Loughborough University in London campus (UK). Her research interests include happiness and well-being, sustainability, social Innovation, creativity, and systemic thinking.

Robert D. Hermanson
a retired architect, has a Masters Degree in Architecture, U. of Penn. Professor Emeritus at the University of Utah College of Architecture and Planning. He has also been a visiting professor at CUA, Washington, DC, Universidad Nacional del Litoral, Santa Fe, Argentina and Université Tunis Carthage, Tunisia.

Julia Hotz
is currently living in Athens, Greece as a Fulbright Scholar. When not teaching English at Athens-Psychico College or volunteering with refugees downtown, Julia enjoys writing and gathering research for an initiative to apply ancient Greek philosophy to modern society.

Søren Harnow Klausen
is Professor of Philosophy at the University of Southern Denmark. He is head of the Values, Welfare and Health Communication research program. Søren Harnow Klausen obtained his PhD1993 at the University of Tübingen, Germany. He was Alexander von Humboldt Research Fellow 2000–2002, member of the Danish Council for Independent Research 2008–2013 and elected member of Science Europe Scientific Advisory Committee 2016. His wide research interests include happiness and wellbeing, value theory, phenomenology, philosophy of mind, social epistemology and philosophy of literature.

Kathy Pui Ying Lo
is Academic Lead of Service Design Mini Centre for Doctoral Training and Lecturer in Visual Communication at Loughborough University. She's an international scholar and educator in service design, experience design, emotional design, and visual communication.

Andrea-Mariana Marian
is currently a PhD student in Sociology at University of Bucharest, Romania. Her main research interest includes happiness studies, with a focus on qualitative methods. She also developed a carrier as a Financial Analyst, holding a leading position in the Finance Department of an international company.

Bryon Martin
is an Assistant Professor of Recreation at Henderson State University, USA. Martin's teaching and research centers on understanding socio-cultural and behavioral aspects of community recreation and sport, service and experiential teaching and learning strategies, and recreation across the lifespan.

Andrew Molas
is a PhD candidate in Philosophy at York University in Toronto. His doctoral research focuses on the role that empathy plays in our engagement with people living with schizophrenia and how cultivating a phenomenological conception of empathy can help reduce stigma and support people in their recovery from mental illness. More broadly, he works on the ethics of care as a normative theory and its application within interpersonal and professional contexts.

Seán Moran
is a philosopher at Waterford Institute of Technology in Ireland, and is happy to be an event leader with the Inter-disciplinary Network. This year, he has become a regular contributor to Philosophy Now, as 'The Street Philosopher'.

Lisa Ortiz
is a Professor of Technical Communication at Metropolitan State University of Denver. Her research interests include media literacy and production, visual communication and Universal Design. Her hobbies include photography, silversmithery and jewellery design.

Ann Shelomi Panditharatne
is currently reading for the PhD at the Faculty of Graduate Studies, University of Colombo, Sri Lanka, and her research interests involve subjective well-being and female labour force participation.

Sheila M. Rucki
is a Professor of Political Science at Metropolitan State University of Denver. Her research centres on applications of neo-Gramscian theory to contemporary political, economic and social issues.

Jane Russell-O'Connor
has a PhD from University of Wolverhampton, UK and has been conducting interdisciplinary research and publishing in landscape history and landscape ecology for over 15 years, primarily in the UK and latterly in Ireland. Her most recent research is that of interdisciplinary research on demesne landscapes. She is currently a lecturer in the Department of Architecture at Waterford Institute of Technology and is supervising three PhD and three research master students. Jane has 23 years teaching experience and has also worked in nature conservation, managing nature reserves. She also runs an environmental and ecological consultancy.

Marie D. Thomas
is Professor Emeritus of Psychology at California State University San Marcos. Her most recent research focused on well-being and positive psychology. Cover design by Amanda Cordell, Graphic Design, HSU.

Introduction

Søren Harnow Klausen, Bryon Martin, Mustafa Cihan Camcı and Sarah A. Bushey

The chapters in this book, which originate from the 2nd global meeting of the Inter-Disciplinary.Net Happiness Project in Budapest, Hungary, 14th-16th March 2016, reflect the complexity of the topic and the need for an interdisciplinary approach. Happiness is studied from many different angles. Some of the chapters are concerned with the general nature or form of happiness, or its relation to human existence in general; others describe how very specific things, like landscapes, classic cars or features of one's home or educational environment, can be conducive to happiness. Some explore the thoughts of ancient or 19th-century philosophers; others employ theories and techniques from contemporary psychology to get a firmer grip on the elusive phenomenon of happiness.

Mustafa Cihan Camci's 'Happiness as the Routine of Everyday Life' uses the Polish award winning director Zbigniew Rybczynski's animated short film *Tango* to explore an ontological notion of happiness. Being immersed in everyday activities and experiencing that one accomplishes a certain goal is a subtle, but very common kind of happiness. In *Tango*, however, the activities are endlessly repeated. According to Camci, this shows how one can become trapped in the hectic routine of everyday life, but also points beyond this routine, as it reveals the more fundamental ontological meaning of happiness. Camci emphasises how happiness is related to the passage of time, which he, with Heidegger, conceives as a process of self-differentiation.

A. Erdem Çifçi's 'Against 'Feeling Good': Aristotle's Concept of Happiness (Eudaimonia)' likewise explores a fundamental, philosophical notion of happiness, which he contrasts with the currently dominant notion of happiness as having pleasurable experiences. Çifçi shows how Aristotle conceived of happiness as the fulfilment of one's nature, and argues that this offers a relevant alternative to the contemporary view. Instead of viewing happiness as an aggregate of momentary and subjective experiences, Aristotle took it to depend on one's general way of being and activities, as well as on external circumstances, though not primarily on material wealth.

Utilitarianism and liberalism are often seen as typical expressions of a modern individualism, which are strongly at odds with the Aristotelian idea of happiness as related to the community and the cultivation of human nature. However, in 'Utility, Liberty, and the State's Duty to Promote Flourishing', Andrew Molas shows how John Stuart Mill argued that the state has a duty to promote collective well-being, and that well-being depends on realizing one's potential and developing a concern for the well-being of others. Though its basic premises are different, the practical implications of Mill's conception are thus not necessarily very different from the Aristotelian, and he does not, at any rate, advocate a form of egotism or argue against collective responsibility and supportive state institutions.

Different concepts and measures of well-being are brought to bear on a practical, empirical question in Ranjeeta Basu and Marie D. Thomas' 'What Makes College Students Happy? A Day Reconstruction Study', which presents the findings from a study of subjective well-being of Californian college students. Basu and Thomas found that life satisfaction is significantly related to grade point average, income, ethnicity, percent of college costs paid by family and hours of sleep. The U-index, measured by the Day Reconstruction Method, is related to income, gender and hours of sleep. Apart from providing clues as to how to make students happier, this also shows that the two measures capture different aspects of well-being. Life satisfaction represents an Aristotelian, *eudemonic* sense of happiness, whereas the U-index measures happiness in a more hedonist, *Benthamite* sense. Basu and Thomas note that the two measures are not very strongly correlated. They further point out that there is a trade-off between hedonist and eudemonic happiness. High pleasure activities may decrease student's sense of achievement. Apart from making the learning process less unpleasant, reminding students of their aspirations and long-term goals may thus also be a way to improve their subjective well-being.

In a unique examination of economic, social, political control, Sheila Rucki and Lisa Ortiz present happiness as a message of hard work, loyalty and self-sacrifice. The 18th Century literary work *Beauty and the Beast* provides an example of happiness in a way Aristotle termed eudaimonia, or flourishing and functioning well in one's nature. Rucki notes that the nobility and social class themes depicted in the fairy tale provide us examples of how the production our self-identity can be understood as an element of happiness. The setting of the literary work provides a historical context from which Rucki draws the parallels between beauty, happiness and the reward for the rejection of social, political, and cultural standards.

Through art therapy techniques, home happiness in terms of creativity, productivity, and fulfilment may obtainable. Emily Corrigan-Doyle, Carolina Escobar-Tello and Kathy Pui Ying Lo's research sheds light on how one's home influences our behaviour, habits, and activity participation and thus, our happiness. A perspective on happiness is gleaned from participant observation in art therapy techniques such visualization, doodling, painting, and the identification of home happiness 'triggers'. The benefits of art therapy techniques provide insight to how positive family time and the roles of people and events in the home create a sense of flow and fulfilling personal happiness.

Sarah Bushey provides a comparative view of happiness and pleasure. In a course offered to college students, Bushey asks students to challenge their own self-awareness of goals and views on *the good life*. Strategies concerning elicitation of student engagement in discussion topics such as student roles in local and world communities, stages of cultural and personal development, and the idea of wealth and material possessions, mindfulness and commodification are discussed. As described by Bushey, educators are faced with the challenge of balancing the view of happiness and pleasure with what they believe and with what the students need, most notably in view of school, career, family and wealth.

The relationship between one's vocation and happiness is described by Andrea-Maraiana Marian and Valeriu Budeanu. Research into happiness at work based on theories of Csikszentmihalyi, among others, provides a framework for discussion. Discovering and knowing the vocation in early life stages may radically change, in good, the destiny of the person, being the best choice for the individual training of this person in their chosen field: vocation becomes the soul of the profession. The vocation is a source of happiness for each person, ensuring continuous happiness, lifting the intensity of happiness. Happiness, in turn, increases the self-confidence and helps overcome the emotions of fear; ensures efficient and effective use of personal resources available. The ingredients of personal satisfaction and fulfilment; ensures personal success; helps in completing high quality work. Happiness also facilitates human relationships, brings more openness and tolerance, and, on the other hand, provides a person with more freedom.

Bryon Martin's paper, 'Classic Cars and Happiness: A Profile of Participants and Their Family, Community and Cultural Health', deals with the classic car fans' activities and the contribution of these activities to individual and communal happiness. In order to discuss this contribution, Martin makes use of both the data collected from a recent study on classic car owners and his qualitative interpretation of classic car recreation. His findings demonstrate that classic car activities such as, collection, cruising in and restoration bring about positive consequences, mostly socialization, preservation of history, and happiness, for the attendants. In addition to the empirical data, Bryon's interpretation shows that classic car recreation is more than just driving a vehicle particularly for the Midwest Americans. It is rather a feeling of the remembrance of the good old days of building up instead of buying a new vehicle which gives rise to sharing a social aim and intimate relationships through generations. Bryon concludes that classic car recreation is associated with rambling through the western tracks of America and thereby a happy feeling of being at home.

Søren Harnow Klausen's paper, 'Happiness and the Structure and Dynamics of Human Life' points out the determinative role of the holistic structures of human lives on the meaning of happy experiences. He argues that this is a dynamic structure of experiences which is not just a synchronic sum of the content of the individual experiences but an interrelated narrative of experiences; a diachronic holistic structure of life. This whole determines the quality of the happiness of a single experience in accordance with its situatedness in this structure. The meaning of an experience is not calculable as if it is an isolated practice. We signify an experience or feeling happy or unhappy if only if we are familiar with the holistic structure of our life. Klausen, indicates the discursive and social nature of this structure as a 'sequence of socially defined events and roles that the individual enacts over time' and concludes that this holistic approach aims at constructing a notion of wellbeing beyond happiness

Bob Hermanson, traces the origins of the western notion of happiness back to the Aristotelian sublime beatitude. He suggests the capitalistic version the Aristotelian understanding of eudaimonia has induced a physical notion of possession, a completion of what is willed, fullness. In addition to this physical interpretation of eudaimonia as fullness, Hermanson points the phenomenological elucidation of Seneca who views happiness as the immediacy of the moment detached from the future projections and expectations. Through Seneca's experience of the aesthetic feeling of the presence of the moment, Hermanson points the possibility of sensing this aesthetic experience by means of both the Japanese gardens and temples and worldly power of the modern cities. The eastern notion of happiness as feeling the immediacy of the moment as the potentiality shows us this experience in a secular form as well as a religious one in which one embraces this potentiality as emptiness to be filled. This embracement of eudaimonia yet remains to oneself.

In 'Earthly Happiness and Heavenly Happiness', Sean Moran associates Aristotle's notion of happiness as an end in itself with Aquinas' felicitas, the earthly happiness via *Pascal's Wager*. The tension between earthly and heavenly happiness, Moran says, can be reconciled through Pascal's recommendation to his unbeliever friends: 'live as if God existed', "veluti si Deus daretur". He advocates Pascal's consequentialist advice which boosts the potential benefits of earthly happiness such as the beatific vision, food, music etc. and accentuates the 'bonus potentialit' of the existence of God for the heavenly benefits. Quoting Robert Burn's lines, Moran shows us the apparent opposition between the earthly happiness and heavenly happiness is blurred in virtuous life.

In her essay titled 'Happiness in Higher Education in Hong Kong: An Anthropology Study', Kelly Chan discusses the emerging identity crisis in Hong Kong due to the transfer of sovereignty from the United Kingdom to China which took place in the late 90s. She connects this emerging crisis to the continuous decline in happiness levels in Hong Kong. The lack of understanding of what happiness consists of in the context of education has contributed to this decline. As an anthropological study, this essay is focused on how university students in Hong Kong define happiness and how it is experienced within higher education.

In 'Re-Embracing Simplicity: An Exploration of Epicurean Happiness', Julia Hotz argues for a revisit to the concept of Epicurean Happiness and offers a look at how the concept has been influenced and changed over time. According to today's definition, *epicurean* means *fond of or adapted to luxury or indulgence in sensual pleasures*. She argues that, in actuality, Epicurus's core tenets opposed luxury and indulgence, contrary to what the modern idea of the concept suggests. Hotz explores the development of Epicurus' philosophy and investigates how his view on happiness became distorted, while also questioning why the original form of epicurean happiness is coming back to the forefront in contemporary life.

Shelomi Panditharatne presents a study investigating the socio-economic factors associated with the subjective well-being of married women in Sri Lanka. Some of the factors considered include their life satisfaction levels and whether or not they work outside the home. Female labour participation in Sri Lanka is one of the lowest in the world, with married women reporting the lowest. Role theory is used to identify the impact on a woman's well-being when assuming multiple roles. The author collected data that included a study of 838 respondents. The data suggests that being employed makes married women significantly less happier than women who are full time homemakers.

In 'The Sublime Landscape', Jane Russell-O'Connor argues that the experience of landscape can make us happy. She traces the history of the term as used by Dutch painters in the 16th century to describe the countryside in terms of scenery that was painted. Russell-O'Connor mentions that landscape was often associated with the sublime, which was not always or usually a tranquil landscape but one of drama, excitement and even danger. Her essay explores the idea of the sublime landscape and how it relates to human happiness. She argues that ultimately, the sublime experience is part of a flourishing life.

Happiness obviously calls for an interdisciplinary approach. It is a multifaceted concept with a long and complex history as well as great actuality. Whatever happiness exactly is – and opinions on this of course differ widely, as will be seen from the articles collected in this volume – it is a complicated and subtle phenomenon. It is sensitive to a large variety of factors – psychological, social, cultural, political, moral, aesthetical etc. – so that a mono-disciplinary approach is almost guaranteed to miss out much that is central to it. Moreover, because happiness is widely considered to be one of the most fundamental values in human life, it also functions as a political ideal, as well as a powerful, but potentially seductive buzzword. Not just happiness as such, but also understandings and representations of happiness constitute an important and challenging field of research. While happiness itself is probably an indisputable good, the concept of happiness has not been immune to abuse. There is much in the way happiness is invoked as a justification for specific policies or used to promote certain ways of life that calls for diagnosis and criticism.

CHAPTER 1

Happiness in the Routine of Everyday Life

Mustafa Cihan Camci

Abstract

In this chapter, I will consider the philosophical notion of happiness as the routine of everydayness. Firstly, we will watch the Polish award winning director Zbigniew Rybczynski's animation: *Tango*. Then, we will discuss the philosophical notion of happiness with reference to the figures' repetitive activities in the film. I will suggest that the figures seem stuck in the same activity and undergo an alienation which let them face the temporal structure of life and become acquainted with the happiness in the ontological sense. I will offer to discuss the repetitive character of routine and the characters' suspension of daily life in this ontological sense. I will refer to some other speakers at the conference. That will match the interdisciplinary attitude of the symposium as well. I will refer to Hermanson's notion of the *Sublime* and make clear that it is the ontological sense of happiness that I am speaking about.[1] I will also consider Gibbs' 'open region' and the 'topology of being' in relation to the temporal sense of everydayness.[2] I will refer to Julia Hotz's 'Tiny House movement' and 'the Busy Trap' and suggest that the sense of temporality can be felt as if one is trapped in the hectic routine of everydayness.[3] I do not provide many quotations and try instead to provoke the attendants (and readers) to imagine the ontological sense of happiness by the use of *Tango*. Avoiding any conclusions, I will merely suggest that the figures remain close to the feeling of the happiness as such yet seem suspended in this closeness, never being able to feel the ontological sense of happiness beyond the everyday life.

Keywords

Tango – happiness as such – everydayness – transcendence

---

1 Robert Hermanson, 'Quo Vadis: Fullness or Emptiness in the Pursuit of Happiness?', in this volume.
2 Paul Gibbs, 'Thinking Education, Happiness and Despair', in this volume.
3 Julia Hotz, 'Re-Embracing Simplicity: An Interdisciplinary Exploration of Epicurean Happiness in the 21. Century', in this volume.

1 Ontological Sense of Happiness as Repetition

Ever since its' beginning, philosophy has been questioning the meaning of being. Despite the limitations of human perception, the philosophers have always tended to grasp the meaning of being as a whole. The meaning of being as a whole is ontology. The ontological attitude of philosophers faces the binary opposition between the pluralistic nature of beings and the oneness of being. This dilemma tempts philosophers to seek the oneness as a transcendence that passes over the many. We can say that Plato is the first philosopher who sees this transcendence as the *epekeina tes ousias*.[4] We still think in Platonic terms when we try to get acquainted with the oneness of the many. Hegel and particularly Heidegger taught us that we can think of this transcendence as the passing over of time. Heidegger says, '*Sein ist die Transzendenz schlechthin*', 'Being is the transcendence pure and simple'.[5] In another lecture, *The Basic Problems of Phenomenology*, he explains the Latin *transcendere* as to step over, to pass over. 'Transcendere means to step over; the transcendens, the transcendent, is *that which oversteps as such* and not that toward which I step over'.[6] Heidegger distinguishes transcendence from immanence with refer to the pre-bias ecstatic structure of temporality.[7] Human beings can be acquainted with the transcendent oneness of ontology in their daily life by virtue of this temporalization of temporality. Heidegger says, 'the *epekeina* belongs to the Dasein's own most peculiar structure of being'.[8] That is to say, the structure of everyday life is temporality. One can imagine the repetitions as the formal structure of what one is doing in the everyday routine. By these repetitions, one can feel the flow of temporality in itself as an unceasing temporalization. The meaning of being as a whole can only be imagined as the self-transcending of temporality.

Thereby, the oneness of the many can be imagined as the temporalization of temporality. In this manner, one can sense the ontological sense of being within her horizon of perception. Time is ecstatic; it is a constant passing over; yet one and the same in itself. It is the threshold of the ontological oneness and the plural structure of beings. In our everyday life, we already experience the passing over of time while we are busy with our daily pursuits. We are concerned

---

4 Jacques Derrida, *Dissemination,* trans. Barbara Johnson (London: Bloomsbury Publishing, 2004), 164.
5 Martin Heidegger, *Sein und Zeit* (Tübingen: Max Niemeyer, 2006), 38.
6 Martin Heidegger, *The Basic Problems of Phenomenology,* trans. Albert Hofstadter (Indianapolis: Indiana University Press, 1982), 299.
7 Ibid.
8 Ibid.

with our tasks. We care accomplishing them. In this concernfull attitude, we subtly calculate the time to do an activity. For instance, if we are playing with a ball, we implicitly estimate the right time to throw the ball and the right time to retrieve it. Time seems to us scattered. We assume that we are experiencing some time to throw the ball and some other time to retrieve it. We perceive time as if it consisted of different parts and ignore its undifferentiated passing over. That is our everyday, concernfull way of living.

Heidegger claimed that in our everyday concern, we are already moving in the being since the ontological sense of being is nothing but temporality. Time to do something is only apparently different from the time to do some other thing. It is time for us. When we are tempted to understand what it is in itself, we come to remember that it is a constant passing over, in Heidegger's words, transcendence pure and simple. Since this transcendence is undifferentiated, time is nothing but the Platonic oneness as *epekeina*. The oneness transcending the many is nothing but an acquaintance for us. Most of the times we are trapped in the routine of our everyday lives and tend to understand time for accomplishing our daily tasks. Happiness in the routine of daily life is the satisfaction of fulfilling our duties. Nevertheless, we never think of the ontological sense of happiness in itself. How can we imagine happiness in the ontological sense? How is this acquaintance possible?

The film we have watched, *Tango*, is an eight minutes animation of a Polish director, Zbigniew Rybczynski.[9] *Tango* is based on the routine activities of thirty-six people in a room. As we noticed, there is an underlying tango rhythm throughout the film. The music subtly reminds us of the holistic structure of the everyday activities by means of its repetitive character. Perhaps, what Søren Klausen means by the holistic pattern of life might be understood in this sense.[10] The routine activities of the inhabitants, which are different from each other, somehow seem undifferentiated and internally connected. Thereby, all the irrelevant characters and activities appear as if they are structured by a formal ideality.

We will come back to this again. Now let us think over what is going on in the film. At the very beginning, we hear tango music and see an empty room. We then see a ball thrown into the room by a boy entering the room and retrieving his lost ball. The boy leaves the room, the ball is thrown into the room again and the boy re-enters the room, repeating his action. Then some other

---

9   *Tango*, dir. Zbigniew Rybczynski, Prague, 1980, viewed 20 November 2015, https://vimeo.com/90339479.

10 Soren H. Klausen, 'Happiness and the Structure and Dynamics of Human Life: Enumerative Approach', in this volume.

characters start entering and leaving the room. They all look preoccupied with their activities. Once the people enter into the room and start their activities, they keep repeating what they do and never end their activity. The characters – the woman who takes care of the baby, the boy throwing his ball in and out of the room and the thief sneaking in and stealing the very same bag over and over – repeat their actions and never pass over to the next action.

Under normal conditions, we expect one to act in order to accomplish a goal and feel happy. It is a subtle sort of happiness; a kind of easiness. One experiences a tacit contentment when one is done with the aimed activity. One is expected to have contentment, an accomplishment for achieving one's goal in a subtle sense. That is how one is happy in one's everyday life. In *Tango* on the other hand, characters' pursuits never come to an end. They cannot complete one pursuit and start a different one. The characters, never being able to pass over to the next activity, are stuck in an endless repetition of the routine of everydayness. In this incompleteness, the happiness seems to be deferred and suspended. In a Platonic sense, the passing over itself, *epekeina*, traps the characters when they are stuck in repetition.

2   The Room Is the *A-topos*

At some point the room is so filled up that the inhabitants look like bees whizzing in the beehive. Nevertheless, none of the rushing figures overlap, since the region is not spatial but temporal. It is probably a kind of place like what Paul Gibbs defines as the 'open region'. As Gibbs says, the Heideggerian 'open region' is both the place of being and where beings can be with one another in a topology of being.[11] The significance of the non-spatial character of the 'open region' is this: The less we care about the place where something happened, the more we care about the happening itself. Happening in this sense reminds us of a special sort of presence. This presence is assumed to be pure since it is abstracted from the spatial limits in this remembrance. Due to its pure temporal character, it leads us to remember the presencing of temporality, *'the transcendence pure and simple'*.

The film reaches its climax when there are 36 characters entering and leaving the small room as if they are the only ones living in that place. The director had to draw and paint about 16.000 cell-mattes for that scene. Despite the *hectic* routine, the figures never touch, never talk and converse to one another.

---

11   Gibbs, 'Thinking Education, Happiness and Despair', in this volume.

One should pay attention to the interpretation of Aristotelian *hexis* as pure potentiality. Hectic routine means a suspended possibility in this sense. The hectic routine represents the deferred, postponed actualization of the final goal as the ontological sense of happiness. *Hexis* as potentiality connotes what is not yet happened but possible. The possibility is the only mode of transcendence. Happiness in the ontological sense, which means transcendence, is remembered in the repetition of the everyday routine. Possibility remains undifferentiated and thus never completed in an actual accomplishment in repetition. Repetition, in this context is similar to the quasi-presence of the formal ideality of everyday life remaining as the undifferentiated differing, as Heidegger's *Selbstunterscheidung* ("self-differentiation") tells us.[12] The undifferentiated differing is the Parmenidean One in this sense. It is Plato's *epekeina* in its repetitive passing over.[13]

Each figure seems to follow her path. However, at the same time they share the same robotic automaticity and the repetitive incompleteness. Without physical contact, their actions look like internally belonging to each other as if they are parts of an unseen holistic structure. The physical space is so small and the flow is so fast that the structure they share cannot be a spatial structure. That is why it is unseen. The structure they share is beyond the physical space. It is a temporal span. The holistic structure of the everyday routine that the figures share tacitly transcends the spatial limits of being in a room. It is a temporal structure.

What is the significance of emphasizing the temporal span as opposed to the spatial space? If we were discussing in a scientific context, one would tell us that Einstein already thought us that time and space are the same. The significance of the temporal understanding as if time is isolated from the spatial dimension is, since we are not physicists, the significance of the meaning of life as happenings. One can recall here what Julia Hotz mentions in her chapter. The 'Tiny House movement' and 'the Busy Trap' can be interrelated in this temporal sense.[14] Trapped in the hectic routine of everyday life, the figures might have a subtle sense of happiness. The figures become alienated to their everyday routine in this busy trap. Trap, in this temporal context means suspension. The figures feel like they are stuck in the temporal flow. This experience makes the figures feel the pure passing over of time. They sense the time as an uncut oneness yet flowing. It is one as self differing. At a special moment,

---

12   Heidegger, *Sein und Zeit*, 129.
13   Derrida, *Dissemination*, 164.
14   Hotz, 'Re-Embracing Simplicity', in this volume.

the figures might beware of the oneness of time as passing over. Nevertheless, this moment of awareness never happens. The figures do not look like they are aware of this oneness as self differing. They rather seem going with the rhythm and never step out of the flow of rhythm. In other words, the figures never transcend the passing over of time to understand the meaning of life.

The passing over of time is transcendence pure and simple. It is nothing but the temporal interpretation of the Platonic *epekeina*. Heidegger calls this '*zeitliches Seiende schlechtin*'.[15] The subtle sense of happiness is the ontological sense of happiness. At the same time as the temporal routine repeats itself as an undifferentiated yet differing potentiality.

The figures' happiness seems incomplete and deferred. This incompleteness makes them feel this temporal structure itself as transcendence. Feeling the temporal transcendence is nothing but feeling the transition as such. The room in the *Tango* is nothing but a place of transition where the *epekeina* can be felt as repetition. Transcending the ordinary sense of happiness, the characters seem comporting to the ontological sense of happiness, happiness as such. Nevertheless, they remain in the suspension of transcending the ordinary happiness and never seem to achieve at the ontological sense of happiness. They start leaving the room one by one in accordance with the music which repeats itself monotonously and reminds us what remains same in repetition. The figures seem close to the ontological sense of happiness but they can never step over the edge. The film ends like a candle fading away … The figures look like trapped within the limits of everydayness.

The suspension of transcending might recall Rilke's lines in 'The Last House'. Rilke says: 'The little village is but a place of transition, expectant and afraid, between two distances, a passageway'.[16]

3 Summary

Ever since Plato, philosophy is understood as an attempt to be acquainted with what is beyond everyday experiences. This Platonic approach is also attributable to the notion of happiness. One can think of being happy in the ordinary sense and happiness as such as the structural form of single happiness. The ordinary sense in this context is the happy experiences of the everyday life. The

---

15 Cihan Camcı, *Heidegger'de Zaman ve Varoluş* (Ankara: Bibliotek Yayınları, 2015), 130.
16 Daniel J. Polikoff, *In the Images of Orpheus: Rilke: A Soul History* (North Caroline: Chiron Publication, 2011), 273.

structural form is the ontological undifferentiated oneness, the idea of happiness. Yet this ontological form can be felt merely while it is differing. This is the ontic sense of happiness.

The idea of happiness is somehow transcendent to the happy experiences of the everyday life. Nevertheless, the difference between this ontological sense of happiness and daily, ordinary happy experiences is not clear. The difference is not a spatial difference. If it were spatial, we would be able to spot it. It is rather a temporal differentiation and belongingness at the same time. It is by virtue of this temporal character that we can feel it while it continues differing. One can sense this differing as passing over. Thus, the happiness in the ontological sense is available as the passage of time. The passage is nothing but the passing over of time. The Platonic attempt to be acquainted with what is beyond everyday activities can be thought as the passing over of time.

The transcendence of the happiness in the ontological sense thereby, can be imagined as the passing over of time. Repetition makes us remember that the temporal differing is an unceasing oneness. Repetition in this sense is the Platonic remembrance. It lets us recall the differing itself as the formal identity of life. The idea of happiness is this formal identity which offers itself throughout the passing over of time. Time is the only possibility to imagine the ontological difference between the idea of happiness and different happy experiences.

Bibliography

Camcı, Cihan. *Heidegger'de Zaman ve Varoluş*. Ankara: Bibliotek Yayınları, 2015.
Derrida, Jacques. *Dissemination*. Translated by Barbara Johnson. London: Bloomsbury Publishing, 2004.
Heidegger, Martin. *Sein und Zeit*. Tübingen: Max Niemeyer, 2006.
Heidegger, Martin. *The Basic Problems of Phenomenology*. Translated by Albert Hofstadter. Indianapolis: Indiana University Press, 1982.
Polikoff, Daniel J. *In the Images of Orpheus: Rilke: A Soul History*. North Caroline: Chiron Publication, 2011.
Tango. Directed by Zbigniew Rybczynski. Prague, 1980. Viewed 20 November 2015. https://vimeo.com/90339479.

CHAPTER 2

Against 'Feeling Good': Aristotle's Concept of Happiness (*eudaimonia*)

A. Erdem Çifçi

Abstract

It is often observed that in the modern period there is an almost perfect consensus on the purpose of human life: being happy regardless of anything that happens. 'Feeling good,' getting pleasure out of whatever it is that one is concerned with, defines the main content of this concept. The modern individual believes that happiness depends on a very particular state of the soul, but the soul is independent of any definite kind of existence or moral law. And he or she assumes that his or her being happy, this distinctive state of the soul, may change from time to time. Aristotle might agree with the first part of this stated purpose—being happy. However, he did not believe that a human being could be happy on his/her own regardless of what happens. Most importantly, Aristotle did not share our concept of happiness. His concept of *eudaimonia*, translated as happiness, also translates as 'human flourishing' or 'well-being'. This concept reminds us of a different kind of happiness which has the sense of fulfilling our nature, and our manner of being happy today does not have to prevail all the time. In this paper, I will try to explain Aristotle's concept of *eudaimonia* and demonstrate the possibilities it offers us in contrast to the modern definition of happiness as 'feeling good'.

Keywords

eudaimonia – feeling good – virtue – activity – *theoria*

How does modern individual understand the concept of happiness? It seems that modern individual gives credit to Stoic motivations believing that he could be happy on his own regardless of what happens. Maybe the large number of books about being happy is evidence for this. Because 'feeling good,' getting pleasure out of whatever it is that one is concerned with, defines the main content of this concept, to be happy seems to be so easy. Nevertheless, modern individual is often sad because he cannot attain such an easy goal. Moreover, he is sad because he is sad, too. He feels bad because he cannot feel good while others apparently do feel good. The modern individual believes that happiness depends on a very particular state of the soul, but the soul is independent of any definite kind of existence or moral law. And he assumes that his being happy, this distinctive state of the soul, may change from time to time. All is 'in the mind'. The individual thinks that he was happy a few minutes ago, and he will be sad shortly after. He can say that "It was the happiest moment of my life, though I didn't know it".[1] His happiness is so fragile. He believes that he could change his life thoroughly by means of changing his ideas. Our manner of being happy today does not have to prevail all the time, however. Aristotle did not share our concept of happiness. His concept of *eudaimonia*, translated as happiness, also translates as 'human flourishing' or 'well-being'. This concept reminds us of a different kind of happiness which has the sense of fulfilling our nature. The concept of *eudaimonia* comes from *eu* (good, like in *eu*thanasia) and *daimonia*, divine beings and destiny or fate. When we have *eudaimonia*, we get pleasure from life; we are virtuous; we exercise our full capacity; we are a bit lucky and we have good divine beings, like Socrates has.[2] This concept reminds us of a development, a becoming excellent, a fulfilling a potentiality.

Aristotle pays attention to the discussion about the content of this concept in his *Nicomachean Ethics*:

> Verbally there is very general agreement; for both the general run of men and people of superior refinement say that it is happiness [that all men seek], and identify living well and doing well with being happy; but with regard to what happiness is they differ, and the many do not give the same account as the wise. For the former think it is some plain and obvious thing, like pleasure, wealth, or honour; they differ, however, from one another—and often even the same man identifies it with different things, with health when he is ill, with wealth when he is poor ...[3]

Aristotle tries to define the main characteristic of happiness on the background of this apparent mess and gives us two of them: self- sufficiency and finality or completeness (*autarkes*). Happiness seems to be desired for its own sake, not for the sake of other goods. Even if we prefer some virtues such as

---

1 Orhan Pamuk, *The Museum of Innocence*, trans. Maureen Freely (New York: Vintage, 2010), 3.
2 Socrates' divine beings are voices warning him about what he should not do.
3 Aristotle, *Nicomachean Ethics. In The Basic Works of Aristotle*. ed. Richard McKeon, trans. W. D. Ross (New York: The Modern Library, 2001), 937.

honour, pleasure or reason for their own sake, we also favour them for happiness at the same time. Happiness means to be a self-sufficient state. Not in a sense of being alone, or living a solitary life outside of community, but in a sense of being in a complete state.[4] And then Aristotle explains further what he understands by happiness.

> [H]uman good turns out to be activity of soul in accordance with virtue, and if there are more than one virtue, in accordance with the best and most complete. But we must add 'in a complete life'. For one swallow does not make a summer, nor does one day; and so too one day, or a short time, does not make a man blessed and happy.[5]

It must be noticed that this good is a kind of activity and it prevails throughout life. It may be thought as an existential state spreads and gives the colour of it all the life instead of a temporary state of mind. It cannot be gained and lost with ease. Perhaps, it must be imagined as a huge performance of an artist pervading all his life. But we should note that Aristotle does not see a perfect resemblance between an artist's work and actions of a virtuous man because of that virtuous activity has to originate from a virtuous character. The moral activity is not enough to make an activity moral. So, he is not interested in merely an activity itself. '*Praise* is appropriate to virtue, for as a result of virtue men tend to do noble deeds ...'.[6] It cannot be reduced to *ataraxia* (a state of tranquillity); it is not an adjective of a passive, sleeping soul. It is a lively, cheerful activity, a continuous state of activity in accordance with virtue. Human being seeks to fulfill their nature in this state, and so can be said to flourish. Placing the contemplation (*theoria*) at the top of this activity in the last book of *Nicomachean Ethics* may seem like a contradiction of his general theory. Nevertheless, it is possible to see virtuous activity and contemplation not as hierarchical but as two dimensions of happiness.

Then what must these activities be if they would be in accordance with virtue? Firstly, we must seek to define what virtue is for Aristotle. He claims that:

> [E]very virtue or excellence both brings into good condition the thing of which it is the excellence and makes the work of that thing be done well; e. g. the excellence of the eye makes both the eye and its work good; for it is by the excellence of the eye that we see well. Similarly the excellence

---

4 Ibid., 941–942.
5 Ibid., 943.
6 Ibid., 950.

> of the horse makes a horse both good in itself and good at running and at carrying its rider and at awaiting the attack of the enemy. Therefore, if this is true in every case, the virtue of man also will be the state of character which makes a man good and which makes him do his own work well.[7]

It is clear that virtue[8] or excellence (*arete*) is an activity, a well doing of a work, and not only confined to human activities. Aristotle mentions further characteristic features of virtue: it is being 'a kind of mean'. It is an ability to choose a mean 'not in the object but relatively to us'.[9] The mean is defined not from an objective criterion but in accordance with our capacity to act. It is not an excess or a deficiency, but just the mean, or 'golden mean'. Aristotle is always a common sense thinker. Nobody can be virtuous without having an ability to evaluate one's power and act in accordance to it. So this attitude needs to a critical thinking, taking account of all dimensions of the problem and it is not easy to solve it. He gives an example of giving money. '[T]o do this to the right person, to the right extent, at the right time, with the right motive, and in the right way, *that* is not for everyone, nor is it easy ...'.[10]

Aristotle believes that pleasure is immanent to the virtuous life, so virtuous life does not need an extra pleasure coming from the praise of others. Thus he does not share our common belief that virtuous people are generally sad or find themselves in difficult positions in this cruel, immoral world. It seems that having a different kind of desire in virtuous activities might be enough to get pleasure coming just from the activity.

He is a so realistic thinker that he claims that we are in need of external goods as well.

> In many actions we use friends and riches and political power as instruments; and there are some things the lack of which takes the lustre from happiness, as good birth, goodly children, beauty; for the man who is very ugly in appearance or ill-born or solitary and childless is not very likely to be happy, and perhaps a man would be still less likely if he had thoroughly bad children or friends or had lost good children or friends by death.[11]

---

7 Ibid., 957.
8 We cut the bread in *virtue* of the knife.
9 Ibid., 958.
10 Ibid., 963.
11 Ibid., 945.

On the other hand, Aristotle might seem more optimistic. We all have a capacity to be virtuous 'Neither by nature, then, nor contrary to nature do the virtues arise in us; rather we are adapted by nature to receive them, and are made perfect by habit'.[12]

What about the other dimension of *eudaimonia*, the activity of *theoria*? Aristotle, in the last part of his *Ethics*, puts the activity of *theoria* at the top of his hierarchy of forms of happiness, and condemns the virtuous life as a secondary class. The critical point here is that happiness should be chosen for itself and never because of another thing[13] and being self-sufficient.[14] All the other activities depend on the others. For example in order to be honourable, we need someone to give us honour, or to be fair we need others again to act on them. It is clear that theoretical activity is more independent activity in comparison to others. In *theoria* we feel ourselves like God by taking part of divine reason. 'If reason is divine, then, in comparison with man, the life according to it is divine in comparison with human life'.[15]

What can we learn from all these thought seeming a bit useless or impractical in this complicated modern life? Can they give any inspiration to us? I'll maintain that they can and try to formulate these inspirations in five entries:

1. First of all, by means of excluding the criteria of 'feeling good', Aristotle might give us an opportunity to examine a concept of happiness that otherwise remains unexamined by the indisputable 'the most significant thing is to feel good about yourself'.
2. Aristotle might prevent us from believing a view that is imposed on us by modern society, viz. that 'everything is in your mind', by reminding us that happiness depends already on external conditions, and that we cannot be happy in spite of great disasters, or in a badly organized society without having proper equipment (Aristotle's approach can thus dismiss our contemporary notion of happiness for the sake of a more genuine notion).
3. Aristotle can teach us that we should care about our general state of mind, or rather our general way of being, that pervades all our life, rather than about our instantaneous joy or sadness, by showing that happiness is not a state of being easily gained or lost.

---

12   Ibid., 952.
13   Ibid., 941.
14   Ibid., 942.
15   Ibid., 1105.

4. By means of his first approach to happiness ('happiness as an activity in accordance with virtue'), by showing that the concept of happiness is not a passive (doing nothing *par excellence*!) kind of serenity, but rather an effort to develop, to perfect oneself or achieve excellence (in a sense of virtue), he might encourage us to live a more productive, more creative, and more active life.
5. By means of his last approach to happiness ('happiness as a contemplation'), Aristotle might remind us that happiness does not require great material wealth, and that it is not too difficult to be happy in an activity of *theoria*, contemplation by thinking about the deep structure of cosmos, harmony and by understanding our temporal existence in it. We could actualize our thinking capacity by engaging in *philosophia*.

Bibliography

Pamuk, Orhan. *The Museum of Innocence*. Trans. Maureen Freely, New York: Vintage, 2010.

CHAPTER 3

Utility, Liberty, and the State's Duty to Promote Flourishing

Andrew Molas

Abstract

This paper explores Mill's understanding of utility and liberty and seeks to gain a better understanding of how we can apply his moral and political theory to improve our social conditions which will allow us to increase the well-being of persons. I outline Mill's understanding of utilitarianism as a moral theory and emphasize the importance of maximizing the well-being of the collective. Although it may appear that his emphasis on maximizing the well-being of others contradicts his emphasis of individual liberty, I demonstrate that these concepts are not in conflict with each other since the preservation of individual liberty is necessary for achieving social utility. I argue that it is the duty of the State to educate its citizens and to ensure that they are responsible agents who are concerned with the interests of others. To achieve this aim the State should foster a society of individuality and 'genius,' it should provide individuals with freedom to decide which goals to pursue in order to increase their overall utility, and it should provide the resources and opportunities necessary for its citizens to achieve them.

Keywords

John Stuart Mill – utilitarianism – liberty – happiness – well-being – welfare – human flourishing – community – State duty

Utilitarianism is a normative theory which holds that actions are morally right if they promote the greatest amount of happiness and morally wrong if they lead to unhappiness.[1] One way of promoting happiness, at least on an individual

---

1 John Stuart Mill, *Utilitarianism*, ed. George Sher (Indianapolis: Hackett Publishing Company, Inc. 2001), 11 ¶2. Given the numerous editions and publications of Mill's primary sources, for clarification purposes I use the "¶" sign to indicate the paragraph Mill is referring to in his

level, is through the pursuit of interests or pleasures which can either be associated with our 'lower' or 'higher' faculties. Pleasures associated with the lower faculties are those associated with 'our bodily needs and requirements, the exercise of which gives rise to pleasures of mere sensation.'[2] For example, whereas drinking a cold lemonade on a warm Summer day constitutes a 'lower pleasure,' attending an academic conference or teaching an undergraduate seminar constitutes a 'higher' pleasure since it exercises my higher faculties. Although humans are capable of experiencing both 'higher' and 'lower' pleasures, Mill maintains that what distinguishes us from non-human animals is that as soon as we become aware of the capacity for mental cultivation, '[we] do not regard anything as happiness which does not include their gratification.'[3] For Mill, a being of higher faculties 'requires more to make him happy ... than one of an inferior type'[4] and despite the fact that there are a privileged few who are able to pursue their interests and entertain these meaningful projects, many people are denied access and/or opportunity to these higher pleasures. According to Mill, part of the reason why some individuals lose their desire to pursue higher aspirations is because they do not have the time or opportunity to indulge in them and, as a result, they 'addict themselves to inferior pleasures' because they are either 'the only ones to which they have access, or the only ones which they are any longer capable of enjoying.'[5] But the problem Mill notices is that once they devote themselves exclusively to the one, they have already become incapable of the other and they gradually lose the capacity for the development of 'nobler feelings.'[6] Our capacity for these nobler feelings, and the desire to improve ourselves, is 'a very tender plant, easily killed, not only by hostile influences, but by mere want of sustenance' and, for most people, this desire to seek a higher mode of life 'speedily dies away if the occupations to which their position in life has devoted them, and the society into which it has thrown them, are not favourable to keeping that higher capacity in exercise.'[7]

---

work. This should allow any reader to locate passages regardless of which edition of *Utilitarianism* or *On Liberty* they are using.

2 John Rawls, *Lectures on the History of Political Philosophy*, ed. Samuel Freeman (Cambridge: Harvard University Press, 2008), 259; Mill, *Utilitarianism*, II ¶4.
3 Mill, *Utilitarianism*, II ¶4.
4 Ibid., II ¶6.
5 Ibid., II ¶7.
6 Ibid., II ¶7.
7 Ibid., II ¶7. This plant metaphor recurs throughout *Utilitarianism* and *On Liberty* and is indicative of the naturalness with which Mill thinks our moral sentiments are. From my understanding, the aim of the individual should be to grow and flourish, to develop one's faculties as much as possible, and to encourage others to do the same. Much like a plant, he maintains that our desire to seek out harmony between our interests and the interests of others is

While it certainly is important for individuals to constantly strive to maximize their potentials and well-being, Mill is careful to emphasize that the standard for the principle of utility is not the agent's own greatest happiness, but 'the greatest amount of happiness altogether' and the only way we can achieve this end is through 'the general cultivation of nobleness of character.'[8] When individuals are unable to find happiness in the pursuit of their higher level interests, the general cause for this feeling of dissatisfaction is that they are caring for nobody but themselves.[9] For those individuals who are entirely self-centred, Mill writes, the 'excitements of life are much curtailed' and that '[n]ext to selfishness, the principal cause which makes life unsatisfactory is want of mental cultivation.'[10] Our quality of life is better when we are not solely egoistic. And in order to experience greater levels of happiness there must be a desire to ground it in the betterment of others.

The reason why we feel an obligation to promote the general happiness of others is due to our social nature and our psychology as social animals.[11] Mill argues that this strive towards promoting general utility is a 'powerful natural sentiment,' and that this 'firm foundation ... of the social feelings of mankind; the desire to be in unity with our fellow creatures' is a powerful principle in human nature which 'tend[s] to become stronger ... from the influences of advancing civilisation.'[12] For Mill, our shared social state is so natural to us that we never conceive ourselves otherwise than as members of a larger body. As a result of our sociality, our inclinations toward wanting to help others ensure that they are actively striving to fully realize their potentials increasingly becomes 'an inseparable part of every person's conception of the state of things which he is born into, and which is the destiny of a human being.'[13]

Within Mill's moral framework, the individual identifies with the collective, and to ensure that our own flourishing occurs it is better to ensure that *everyone* is able to succeed as much as possible. While he has been focusing primarily on what individuals can do on a personal level, Mill shifts his focus in *On Liberty* to the role of the State and how the State can implement these kinds of principles into practice. Although it is important to note that Mill does not

---

      'deeply rooted' in our shared human nature, and with careful cultivation we can produce a society which is more hospitable to all (Mill, *Utilitarianism*, III ¶11).

8   Mill, *Utilitarianism*, II ¶9.
9   Ibid., II ¶13.
10   Ibid., II ¶13.
11   Ibid., III ¶1.
12   Ibid., III ¶10.
13   Ibid., III ¶10.

offer us a prescriptive account of *how* the State should structure its institutions to create an environment that is conducive to human flourishing, he does explain that a necessary component for maximizing utility is the preservation of individual liberty.

One of the main obstacles which restrict the growth of individual liberty is 'the tyranny of the prevailing opinion and feeling' and the tendency of society 'to impose ... its own ideas and practices as rules of conduct ... to fetter the development, and ... [to] prevent the formation, of any individuality not in harmony with its ways.'[14] To overcome the tyranny of the State, Mill argues that there are three types of liberties that need to be protected: the liberty of thought, the freedom of association, and the liberty of tastes and pursuits, which involves the freedom for us to create and follow plans of life that 'suit our own character; of doing as we like ... without impediment' as long as we do not harm others.[15]

While some of the sources of suffering which prevents individuals from maximizing their utility and promoting the welfare of others are self-inflicted, and include things such as 'gross imprudence' or 'ill-regulated desires' (e.g. reckless gambling), one significant source of the 'vicissitudes of fortune' that inhibits individual flourishing is the presence of 'bad or imperfect social institutions.'[16] Due to customs and conventions, Mill maintains that Western society has spent a significant amount of effort to compel individuals to conform to its notions of social excellence.[17] But while he acknowledges that customs are important to the extent that they help establish certain rules and conduct which help guide our behaviour (e.g. legal systems), conforming to customs, at the expense of losing one's individuality, does not develop in us any of the qualities which are the 'distinctive endowment of a human being' because our unique faculties of judgment and moral preference 'are exercised only in making a choice' and anyone who does anything *because* it is the custom 'makes no choice' at all.[18]

Reaffirming the natural imagery once more, Mill maintains that human nature 'is not a machine to be built after a model, and set to do exactly the work prescribed for it' but rather it is 'a tree, which requires to grow and develop itself on all sides' without interference.[19] This notion of growth is significant because

---

14   John Stuart Mill, *On Liberty and Other Writings—Cambridge Texts in the History of Political Thought*, ed. Stefan Collini (New York: Cambridge University Press, 1989), I ¶5.
15   Mill, *On Liberty*, I ¶12.
16   Mill, *Utilitarianism*, II ¶14.
17   Mill, *On Liberty*, I ¶14.
18   Ibid., III ¶3.
19   Ibid., III ¶4.

it is only the 'cultivation of individuality' which produces 'well-developed human beings' who are capable of promoting the interests of others in the name of maximizing general utility.[20] Rather than thwarting their growth, we need to encourage others to develop and realize their potentials because it can lead to progress in society which would ultimately lead to *improvements* in the conditions of society which are more equitable and accessible to everyone. We need persons of genius 'to discover new truths ... to commence new practices, and [to] set the example of more enlightened conduct, and better taste and sense in human life' but these individuals 'can only breathe freely in an atmosphere of freedom' and, as a result, it is necessary for society 'to preserve the soil in which they grow.'[21]

The problem Mill identifies in modern society is that individuals are 'lost in the crowd,' their voices are drowned out by public opinion, and their choices are heavily influenced by customs and conventions.[22] If individuality and creative genius are stifled by the influence of the public opinion, society 'will be little the better for their genius' because these individuals will not be able to use their talents to increase the general utility of society as a whole.[23] Mill wants us to embrace our individuality, and to think critically, and although the standards established by custom enforce a uniformity of thought and action, he notes that different persons require different conditions for their 'spiritual development' and that the same things that are conducive or helpful to the growth of one person may serve as a hindrance to another person.[24] Just as there is a diversity in preferences and tastes amongst individuals, Mill maintains that there should be 'different experiments of living.'[25] When a society stifles individuality, or if the structure of its institutions prevents people from freely pursuing their own interests, Mill claims that 'there is wanting one of the principal ingredients of human happiness, and quite the chief ingredient of individual and social progress.'[26] The deprivation of individuality results in stagnation—the antithesis of progress—but by celebrating difference and diversity we can collaborate and achieve greater things.[27]

---

20 Ibid., III ¶10.
21 Ibid., III ¶11.
22 Ibid., III ¶13.
23 Ibid., III ¶11.
24 Ibid., III ¶14.
25 Ibid., III ¶1.
26 Ibid., III ¶1.
27 Ibid., III ¶17.

For Mill, the concept of liberty involves autonomy, freedom of choice, and an equal access of opportunity to live a meaningful life. If individuals are allowed to flourish by having the liberty to pursue any kind of life they wish in the name of promoting utility (for themselves *and* others), then society (as a collection of individuals) flourishes as well. Given these basic liberties Mill wishes to preserve against impediment from the State, individuals have a great responsibility to themselves to fulfil their potentials as much as possible.[28] But instead of viewing his theory of liberty as one which promotes 'selfish indifference' where individuals are not concerned with the well-being of others unless their own interests are involved, once again Mill emphasizes the importance of the collective responsibility to maximize general utility. Because of our social nature, he maintains that human beings owe it to each other help to distinguish the good things from the bad things and that we should encourage others to choose aims and projects that will promote the best overall utility and avoid things which decrease it.[29] Since we are capable of identifying our aims with those of others we should be 'forever stimulating each other to increased exercise of their higher faculties' and we should be directing their aims and feelings that are 'wise instead of foolish, elevating instead of degrading ...'[30]

In addition to the duty to maximize our potentials and to promote the wellbeing of others, we also have a duty to future generations to ensure that we instil in them the proper moral virtues necessary for them to develop as rational, responsible agents capable of propagating these feelings of unity and utility. Mill argues that our current generation is responsible for educating future generations and ensuring that certain social standards are set in place for their growth. But although we cannot make the future generation perfectly moral and free of vice, our aim should be to make the next generation 'as a whole, as good as, and a little better than, [ourselves]' and if a society lets any considerable amount of its members to grow up without having this feeling and desire to promote the social good, then that society has itself to blame for the consequences.[31] Not only do we require the proper institutional foundation to secure this kind of future for society, but we also require an attitude adjustment on the personal level. As Mill explains, attitudes such as anti-social tendencies, malice, envy, resentment of others, greed, and pride are 'moral vices' which constitute a 'bad and odious moral character' that undermines social cohesion.[32]

---

28   Ibid., IV ¶6.
29   Ibid., IV ¶4.
30   Ibid., IV ¶4.
31   Ibid., IV ¶11.
32   Ibid., IV ¶6.

Despite the range of inequalities which exclude portions of our society from fully realizing their potentials, Mill argues that most of these 'great positive evils of the world' and "[a]ll the grand sources ... of human suffering" are in a great degree 'conquerable' by human care and effort.[33] Although minimizing these sources of suffering is a long process (factors such as poverty, disease, and other inequalities), Mill remains hopeful that 'the wisdom of society' combined with the 'good sense and providence of individuals' will allow us to elevate the well-being of others in our community.[34] Even if we cannot eliminate these negative factors completely we can still improve our current state of affairs. Mill is suggesting that there is a collective responsibility to improve the state of society by making it more accessible to everyone and full of more opportunities. To do this we must not infringe upon the rights of others and we should encourage others to realize their full potentials as much as possible.

It is important to note that, for Mill, we cannot force people into adopting a certain mode of life. In the name of promoting liberty we have to allow individuals to possess the right to decide based on their preferences and to hold individuals responsible for the outcome of their decisions. For that reason, Mill argues that society between human beings is 'manifestly impossible on any other footing than that the interests of all are to be consulted. Society between equals can only exist on the understanding that the interests of all are to be regarded equally.'[35] However, not all interests have the same weight or value and some interests should be actively pursued over others. For instance, a life devoted to education is more favourable than a life devoted to gambling. This fact should not detract from the viability of either the principle of utility or the principle of liberty. Nevertheless, no matter how we try to better ourselves the aim of maximizing our potentials in the name of increasing general utility should be the goal. We should not deny individuals the opportunity to live their lives as they see fit, even if it goes against the standards established by custom. If someone chooses interests that do not allow him to realize his full potential, that individual 'may be to us an object of pity ... [but] we shall not treat him like an enemy of society.'[36] If we are serious about preserving individual liberty the possibility for failure must be present. The State should do everything within its justified authority to prevent its citizens from going astray, but we have to allow individuals to make their own decisions.

---

33 Mill, *Utilitarianism*, II ¶14.
34 Ibid., II ¶14.
35 Ibid., III ¶10.
36 Mill, *On Liberty*, IV ¶7.

In regards to the State's role in developing its citizens into agents who strive to realize the greater good collectively, Mill argues that 'the peculiar training of a citizen' involves taking them out of 'the narrow circle of personal ... selfishness' and to accustom them 'to the comprehension of joint interests, the management of joint concerns—habituating them to act from public ... motives, and guide their conduct by aims which unite instead of isolating them from one another.'[37] Instead of imposing its own will and interests on the people, the State should create policies which 'aids and stimulates individual exertion and development' and that 'mischief begins when ... it substitutes its own activity for theirs' and prevents individuals from realizing their fullest potentials.[38] For Mill, stability of the State depends on the citizens which comprise it and whenever the State 'compels all characters to fashion themselves upon the model of its own'[39] it 'postpones the interests of their mental expansion and elevation' and, therefore, prevents the achievement of general utility.[40] By preventing individuals to flourish, the State 'dwarfs its men ... [and] will find that with small men no great thing can really be accomplished' and that 'the perfection of machinery to which it has sacrificed everything will in the end avail it nothing.'[41]

While Mill realizes the significance of the State's role in the moral and political education of its people to prepare them to care about the collective good, he argues, '[t]he present wretched education, and wretched social arrangements, are the only real hindrance to its being attainable by almost all.'[42] Society is partly to blame for the inability of some to pursue higher interests, and as a result, cooperation of all is needed to ensure the happiness of the collective. If we ensure that the proper foundation is in place it would allow us to continue to pursue the higher pleasures rather than defaulting to the simpler pleasures because they are more accessible. A broken system will prevent many from achieving their potential. But every step we take towards 'levelling those inequalities ... between individuals or classes' will result in 'an improving state of the human mind' which is geared toward development and progress and unity with others.[43]

---

37 Ibid., v ¶19.
38 Ibid., v ¶23.
39 Ibid., I ¶5.
40 Ibid., v ¶23.
41 Ibid., v ¶23.
42 Mill, *Utilitarianism*, II ¶12.
43 Ibid., III ¶10

Since we must remain impartial and take everyone's unique interests into account, Mill argues that in order to make this ideal state a reality our laws and social arrangements 'should place the happiness ... of every individual, as nearly as possible in harmony with the interest of the whole' and that we should use the influence of education and opinion 'to establish in the mind of every individual an indissoluble association between his own happiness and the good of the whole.'[44] By creating a supportive society in accordance with the principles of liberty and utility, Mill maintains that these '[g]enuine private affections and a sincere interest in the public good, are possible ... to every rightly brought up human being.'[45] Although Mill's project is an ambitious one, he maintains that if we use the whole force of education, of institutions, and of opinion, 'directed ... to make every person grow up from infancy surrounded ... by the profession and the practice of it'[46] there is absolutely no reason why these feelings of utility and social cohesion should not be 'the inheritance of every one born in a civilised country.'[47] Systemic changes at the foundational level is the only way for a State to be grounded upon the principles of equality, liberty, and utility. And while it may be difficult to implement completely, I think Mill believes that the transformation is certainly possible. It simply requires that we view ourselves as progressive agents who actively seek to improve the conditions and well-being of others.

Bibliography

Mill, John Stuart. *On Liberty and Other Writings—Cambridge Texts in the History of Political Thought.* Edited by Stefan Collini. New York: Cambridge University Press, 1989.

Mill, John Stuart. *Utilitarianism.* 2nd ed. Edited by George Sher. Indianapolis: Hackett Publishing Company, Inc. 2001.

Rawls, John. *Lectures on the History of Political Philosophy.* Edited by Samuel Freeman. Cambridge: Harvard University Press, 2008.

---

44   Ibid., II ¶18.
45   Ibid., II ¶14.
46   Ibid., III ¶10.
47   Ibid., II ¶14.

CHAPTER 4

What Makes College Students Happy? A Day Reconstruction Study

Ranjeeta Basu and Marie D. Thomas

Abstract

In this paper, we discuss subjective well-being of college students in a mid-size public comprehensive university in California. We discuss two measures of well-being: overall life satisfaction and the U-index calculated using the Day Reconstruction Method. Although overall life satisfaction and the U-index tend to be fairly correlated they do capture different aspects of subjective well-being. According to Kahneman and Krueger, factors like ethnicity, income, and education are more closely related to overall life satisfaction than to the U-index. In addition, they suggest that adaptation to changes in our life circumstances as measured by overall life satisfaction may be different from the U-index. We examine the relationships between these variables in the case of college students. Gender, income and hours of sleep are the most significant factors that related to the U-index. On the other hand, life satisfaction is significantly related to GPA, household income, race/ethnicity, percentage of college costs paid by family and hours of sleep. We explore differences in how students choose to spend their time and the U-index associated with different activities to explain our findings. These findings can have important implications for how we attend to the needs of different sections of the student population to help them succeed.

Keywords

subjective well-being – college students – time use – Day Reconstruction Method – U-index – life satisfaction

1   Introduction

At the January 2016 annual meeting of the Association for American Colleges and Universities, a session was organized by the non-profit group Bringing Theory to Practice to consider the questions, 'What can colleges do to promote their students' well-being?' and 'Why is student well-being an outcome that colleges should pay attention to?' Research discussed in these sessions reported, for example, that well-being differs by race, and such demographic variables must be taken into account when considering how to improve well-being on college campuses.[1]

We have been interested in the topic of college student well-being for several years. In this paper, we present research describing two measures of subjective well-being in college students at a mid-size public comprehensive university in California.

The first assessment was overall life satisfaction, the most common way to measure subjective well-being. For example, the World Values Survey asks participants from 81 countries: 'All things considered, how satisfied are you with your life as a whole these days?' Such a question is asking participants to make a retrospective judgment about how their life measures up against their aspirations and goals. The validity of this type of question is mixed. On the one hand, research has shown that are influenced by the context within which the question is asked and the affective state of the respondent.[2] On the other hand, overall life satisfaction measures are highly correlated with relevant physiological,[3] psychological/neurological,[4] and economic[5] variables.

The Day Reconstruction Method (DRM), developed by Kahneman et al.,[6] is another way to measure subjective well-being. It relies on trying to recall, as accurately as possible, experienced affect from the previous day. Respondents are asked to divide the preceding day into short episodes. For each episode, they report what they were doing (from a list of activities), with whom they were interacting, and how they were feeling. From this information, it is possible to calculate a measure called the U-index which indicates the percentage of time the respondent spends in an unhappy state. This measure has been found to be

---

[1] Ellen Wexler, 'Should Colleges Measure Well-Being?', *Inside Higher Ed*, January 21, 2016, Viewed on 21 January, 2016, https://www.insidehighered.com/news/2016/01/21/what-colleges-can-do-measure-and-promote-students-well-being.
[2] Norbert Schwarz and Gerald L. Clore, 'Mood, Misattribution, and Judgments of Well-Being: Informative and Directive Functions of Affective States', *Journal of Personality and Social Psychology* 45.3 (1983): 513–523.
[3] Sheldon Cohen, et al., 'Emotional Style and Susceptibility to the Common Cold', *Psychosomatic Medicine* 65.4 (2003): 652–657.
[4] Heather Urry, et al., 'Making a Life Worth Living', *Psychological Science* 15.6 (2004): 367–372.
[5] Ada Ferrer-i-Carbonell, 'Income and Well-Being: An Empirical Analysis of the Comparison Income Effect', *Journal of Public Economics* 89.5-6 (2005): 997–1019.
[6] Daniel Kahneman, et al., *A Survey Method*, 1776–1780.

correlated to the more difficult to implement Experience Sampling method.[7] The DRM has been used worldwide,[8] primarily studying working and older adults. Few studies have used college student samples;[9] none have focused on well-being and time use.

Although overall life satisfaction and the U-index tend to be fairly correlated, they do capture different aspects of subjective well-being. According to Kahneman and Krueger, factors like ethnicity, income, and education are more closely related to overall life satisfaction than to the U-index.[10] In addition, they suggest that adaptation to changes in life circumstances as measured by overall life satisfaction may be different from the U-index. In our study, we examine the relationships between these variables in a sample of college students. Preliminary studies on college students have pointed to a link between overall life satisfaction and academic retention and academic performance.[11] Another study on overall life satisfaction and satisfaction across different domains found a significant difference in satisfaction with school and self by race.[12]

Another way to think about the difference between these two measures is to link it to different conceptualizations of happiness. According to Bentham, happiness is based on the pursuit of pleasure or the absence of pain. In contrast, Aristotle's notion of eudemonia defines happiness as the pursuit of excellence or striving to achieve your full human potential. Nussbaum argues that neither conceptualization of happiness is complete because sometimes human beings are happy to engage in activities that pursue excellence or a

---

7   Samantha Dockray, et al., 'A Comparison of Affect Ratings Obtained with Ecological Momentary Assessment and the Day Reconstruction Method', *Social Indicators Research* 99.2 (2010): 269–283.
8   Jose´ Luis Ayuso-Mateos, et al., 'Multi-Country Evaluation of Affective Experience: Validation of an Abbreviated Version of the Day Reconstruction Method in Seven Countries', *PLOS ONE* 8.4 (2013): 1–8.
9   Karen Brans, Iven Van Mechelen, and Bernard Rimé, 'To Share, or Not to Share? Examining the Emotional Consequences of Social Sharing in the Case of Anger and Sadness', *Emotion* 14.6 (2014): 1062–1071; Michael Daly, et al., 'Self-Control and its Relation to Emotions and Psychobiology: Evidence from a Day Reconstruction Method Study' *Journal of Behavioral Medicine* 37 (2014): 81–93; Sanjay Srivastava, Kimberly M. Angelo, and Shawn R. Vallereux, 'Extraversion and Positive Affect: A Day Reconstruction Study of Person–Environment Transactions', *Journal of Research in Personality* 42 (2008): 1613:1618.
10 Daniel Kahneman and Anne Krueger, *Developments in the Measurement*, 3–24.
11 Michael B. Frisch, et al., 'Predictive and Treatment Validity of Life Satisfaction and the Quality of Life Inventory', *Assessment* 12 (2005): 66–78.
12 Keith Zullig, Eugene S. Huebner, and Scott M. Pun, 'Demographic Correlates of Domain-Based Life Satisfaction Reports of College Students', *Journal of Happiness Studies* 10 (2009): 229–238.

life of virtue even if it brings them pain.[13] On the other hand, living a life of excellence without any pleasure cannot be seen as happiness either. The life of a student exemplifies this contradiction very well. In the pursuit of higher education, students will often have to work hard and make many sacrifices which might not bring them pleasure in the Benthamite sense, but such behaviour might induce eudemonia. In this paper we examine this contradiction by looking at overall life satisfaction as a proxy for eudemonia and the U-index as a proxy for Bentham's notion of happiness. Students can have a high degree of life satisfaction if they feel like they are achieving their goals as evidenced by the correlation of life satisfaction to GPA. At the same time their fairly high U-index indicates that the actions needed to reach their goals are not necessarily pleasurable on a day to day basis. In making decisions on how to spend their time, students must grapple with the trade-off between activities that are pleasurable and activities that help them achieve their academic goals.

2 Method

We conducted an online survey consisting of items measuring well-being, time use, and aspirations. A variety of demographic data were also collect. Respondents were university students from the Psychology Department Human Participant Pool (who received credit for their participation and were mostly in their first or second year of college) and students from a set of selected upper-division courses in Economics, Psychology, Human Development, Sociology, Geography, Math, Biology, and Business. After adjusting for missing observations and other reporting errors, the final sample consisted of 572 completed surveys.

Mean age was 24 years old ($SD = 4.4$). Students were enrolled in an average of 13 units of class work ($SD = 2.8$), with a mean grade point average (GPA) of 3.09 out of 4 ($SD = .52$). Approximately 68% of the sample is female, which corresponds very closely to the institution's student population. Most of the sample reported race/ethnicity as Caucasian (46%); another 30% reported being Hispanic, and 10% were Asian American. Most of the respondents were from the following majors: Human Development (22%), Psychology (21%), Business

---

[13] Martha Nussbaum, 'Mill between Aristotle and Bentham', *Economics and Happiness: Framing the Analysis*, ed. Luigino Bruni and Pier Luigi Porta (Oxford: Oxford University Press, 2007), 170–183.

(11%) and Economics (10%). About 66% of respondents reported that, in addition to studying at the university, they were employed at an outside job (M hours worked = 23, SD =10). A slight majority of respondents (52%) live at home with their parents.

While the online survey measured several aspects of well-being, in this paper we focus on the two measures of subjective well-being discussed earlier: overall life satisfaction and DRM. The life satisfaction item was 'Taking all things together, how satisfied are you with your life as a whole these days?' This was measured with a four-point scale: Very satisfied (4), Satisfied (3), Not very satisfied (2), and Not at all Satisfied (1). For the DRM, respondents were asked to recreate the previous day's activities by dividing the time spent awake into episodes ranging from 20 minutes to 2 hours long. Respondents then answered questions about what they were doing and with whom during each of the episodes. They also rated ('How did you feel during this episode?') several positive and negative affective states (impatient for it to end, competent/confident, tense/stressed, happy, depressed/blue, interested/focused, affectionate/friendly, calm/relaxed, irritated/angry, tired) on a 7-point scale with Not at all and Very strongly as endpoints. The U-index was calculated by determining the most pronounced affective state in each episode and weighting it by the amount of time spent in the episode. The higher the U-index, the more time spent in an unpleasant state.

3 Results and Discussion

While the correlation between overall life satisfaction and the U-index was statistically significant (r = -0.18) it is still fairly small suggesting that it is worthwhile to consider each of these measures separately. Students in our sample spent, on average, 23% of their time in an unhappy state. Kahneman et al. used the DRM approach to calculate the U-index for a sample of 909 working women in Texas and found that the women spent a mean of 17.7% of their time in an unhappy state.[14]

As indicated in Table 4.1, the correlations between the U-index and overall life satisfaction with other demographic and academic variables such as hours worked and number of units enrolled were not statistically significant. In addition, factors such as living situation, employment status and choice of major were not significantly related to life satisfaction or the U-index.

---

14 Daniel Kahneman, et al., *A Survey Method*, 1776–1780.

TABLE 4.1 Correlations between U-index, life satisfaction, and demographic/academic variables

Variable	Correlation with U-index	Correlation with life satisfaction
Grade point average	0.017	0.121[a]
Hours worked per week	-0.076	-0.002
Number of units enrolled	0.029	-0.006
Hours slept night before	-0.286*	0.109*
% of college costs paid by family	0.029	0.126*

[a] Statistically significant

GPA was significantly related to overall life satisfaction but not to the U-index. The positive relationship between overall life satisfaction and academic performance confirms the findings of other studies. It also confirms our hypothesis that overall life satisfaction is more of a measure of eudemonic notions of happiness. The percentage of college costs paid by family is another factor that was positively correlated to life satisfaction but not the U-index. Immediate factors such as the number of hours slept the preceding night were significantly correlated with life satisfaction and U-index although the correlation with the U-index is higher.

Time use. The DRM approach allows us to examine time use and the affect experienced when engaging in different activities during the day. Table 4.2 below provides the ranking of activities for the full sample by the U-index. Similar to earlier studies, leisure or discretionary activities such as watching TV or making love have the lowest U-index, while activities that are considered obligatory, like schoolwork and commuting, have the highest U-index. Using a sample of college students, Waterman classified activities along two dimensions: effort and pleasure.[15] He classified low effort but high pleasure activities such as watching TV as hedonic activities and high effort and high pleasure activities such as exercise as eudemonic activities. Attending class is an activity that requires much effort and would, therefore, be considered as eudemonic, but our results show that it is not an activity that generates pleasure. Since

---

15 Alan Waterman, 'When Effort is Enjoyed: Two Studies of Intrinsic Motivation for Personally Salient Activities', *Motivation and Emotion* 29 (2005): 165–188.

TABLE 4.2 Ranking of activities by U-index

Activity	% of Sample	Time spent (Minutes)	U-index
Making Love	8.60%	119.86	0.02
Watching TV	22.20%	122.54	0.08
Playing	5.20%	138.10	0.10
Shopping	12.10%	102.61	0.14
Talking	40.90%	163.68	0.14
Exercising	9.80%	114.18	0.14
Eating	36.00%	79.50	0.16
Cooking	14.20%	76.57	0.17
Parenting	9.30%	193.49	0.17
Listening to Music	7.70%	81.07	0.21
Sleeping	22.00%	205.25	0.25
Clubs	2.10%	143.58	0.25
Housework	14.30%	116.43	0.26
Praying	4.50%	106.15	0.27
Working	22.40%	249.47	0.28
Grooming	33.20%	62.89	0.30
Reading	7.70%	87.98	0.32
Commuting	30.90%	77.32	0.34
Schoolwork	38.60%	183.37	0.34
In Class	31.30%	160.88	0.35

the DRM approach has not been used to study time use in a sample of college students, the result that students spend an average of 35% of time in class in an unhappy state is a new insight.

In the next section we focus on differences in well-being by gender, race and household income.

Gender. In our sample, women and men differed significantly on several demographic variables. Women had a higher mean GPA (Mwomen = 3.14, SD = .50; Mmen = 2.96, SD = .54; $t(567)$ = 3.90, $p < .01$), worked fewer hours per week (Mwomen = 21.65, SD = 9.15; Mmen = 25.25, SD = 11.01; $t(375)$ = 3.24, $p < .01$), and were enrolled in more units (Mwomen = 13.3, SD = 2.65; Mmen = 12.62, SD = 2.87; $t(567)$ = 2.77, $p < .01$). Men tended to have more household income, with 44% of men but only 29% of women in the highest income category.

TABLE 4.3 Activities by gender and U-index

	Women	Men
Activities with lowest U-index	Making love (.03)	Making love (.00)
	Watching TV (.07)	Watching TV (.10)
Activities with highest U-index	Working (.31)	Housework (.30)
	Reading (.33)	In class (.30)
	Schoolwork (.33)	Reading (.31)
	Grooming (.34)	Schoolwork (.39)
	In class (.38)	
	Commuting (.40)	

TABLE 4.4 Household income, U-index, and life satisfaction

Household Income	% of sample	U-index	Life satisfaction
Less than $20,000	36	0.27	2.99
$20,000 to $60,000	30	0.22	3.08
More than $60,000	34	0.21	3.17

Women and men did not differ significantly in U-index (Mwomen = .25, SD = .29; Mmen = .2, SD = .28) or in overall life satisfaction (Mwomen = 3.1, SD = .61; Mmen = 3.06, SD = .76).

The ranking of activities by men and women reveal some interesting differences. Table 4.3 below shows the activities with the lowest U-indexes (.10 and below) and highest U-indexes (.30 and above). Commuting is far more unpleasant for women (0.40) then for men (0.21), as is grooming (.34 versus .19). These U-indexes are significantly different.

Race. In our sample, white students were enrolled in the highest amount of units and have the highest GPAS. Number of hours worked per week did not vary significantly among the three groups. White and Asian students were distributed toward both ends of the income scale, while the majority of Hispanic student were distributed toward the low-income end.

There were significant differences in life satisfaction across the different racial/ethnic groups, with Asian American students reporting the lowest

TABLE 4.5 Activities by household income and U-index

	Less than $20,000	$20,000 to $60,000	More than $60,000
Activities with lowest U-index	Making love (.05) Watching TV (.07)	Making love (.00) Watching TV (.06)	Making love (.00) Exercising (.10)
Activities with highest U-index	Commuting (.34) Schoolwork (.37) Housework (.37) Working (.37) Grooming (.38) In class (.43)	In class (.30) Schoolwork (.30) Commuting (.33)	Reading (.30) Sleeping (.30) Commuting (.34) Schoolwork (.35)

overall life satisfaction (MH = 3.12, SD = .676; MW = 3.17, SD = .627; MAA = 2.88, SD = .662; $F(2, 490)$ = 4.89, $p < .01$). Zullig, Huebner and Pun found that non-white students had a significantly lower satisfaction with self and school compared to white students.[16] The groups did not differ significantly by U-index.

We will not address differences in activities because the Asian American group was small enough that there were few respondents in each of the activities.

Household Income. As indicated in Table 4.4, several significant differences were found for the three household income groups. GPA increased with income (Mlow = 3.03, SD = .52; Mmiddle = 3.08, SD = .48; Mhigh = 3.15, SD = .53; $F(2, 564)$ = 3.10, $p < .05$). Perhaps not surprisingly, U-index decreased with income while overall life satisfaction increased with income. The differences in life satisfaction were statistically significant ($F(2, 564)$ = 3.29, $p < .05$), while the differences in the U-index were close to statistical significance ($F(2, 564)$ = 2.71, $p < .07$).

The pattern of activities ranked by U-index showed interesting differences. Table 4.5 shows the activities with the lowest U-indexes (.10 and below) and highest U-indexes (.30 and above).

While these differences were not statistically significant, they do reflect a disparity in ranking of activities across the income groups. Being in class is much more unpleasant for low income students (0.42) compared to middle

---

16 Keith Zullig et al, *Demographic Correlates*, 229–238.

and high income students (0.29). Working is much more unpleasant for low income students (0.37) compared to middle (0.23) and high income students (0.21). Housework is much more unpleasant for low income students (0.37) as compared to middle income (0.19) and high income students (0.17). Given that lower income students also have a lower GPA, they are more likely to experience lower life satisfaction and, therefore, have lower eudemonic happiness. They also tend to have a higher in-class U-index suggesting that their learning experience is less pleasurable as well. We contend that these factors work together to decrease the academic success of lower income students. Such students seem to experience the learning process differently and would require different kinds of interventions to increase academic success.

4 Conclusion

How can we use the findings of our study to make students happier? Our findings suggest that life satisfaction is significantly related to: GPA, income, race/ethnicity, percent of college costs paid by family and hours of sleep, and the U-index is related to: income, gender and hours of sleep. One clear implication of these findings is that students could improve their happiness in both the Benthamite and eudemonic sense by sleeping more hours. Perhaps scheduling classes that start later in the day versus early in the morning might be one policy recommendation flowing from this result. Second, our findings suggest that income matters. Therefore, increasing scholarships or decreasing tuition would not only increase academic performance but would also improve student well-being. Third, female and lower income students experience classroom learning as more unpleasant than do other students; this suggests that the same pedagogy does not work for all students. If we want all students to be successful and experience the learning process in a positive way versus a chore they somehow must get through, we need ways to teach more effectively to these populations. Fourth, students of colour have lower levels of life satisfaction than white students which again suggests that we need to provide targeted support to different groups of students and not assume that one size fits all.

Our findings also suggest that the U-index is related to the kinds of activities students engage in and how students choose to spend their time. While at first glance it might appear that one way to lower the U-index and make students happier might be for them to spend more time watching television and making love, this might also decrease their sense of achievement and hence their eudemonic happiness. In other words, low effort and high pleasure activities might improve happiness in a Benthamite sense but not in a eudemonic sense. Instead, perhaps we need to look for ways to remind students about their aspirations and their reasons for working towards a university degree, especially at those times when the learning process is particularly arduous (e.g., midterm and final exams). Another approach might be to encourage students to study in groups because interacting with others does reduce the unpleasantness of unpleasant activities. As mentioned earlier, adopting teaching techniques that help students find joy in the learning process might be another way to improve their well-being and lower their in-class U-index. Such techniques include, but are not limited to, learning by discovery, being aware of where students are in terms of preparation and pitching the course difficulty level so that it challenges students without frustrating them, and including mindfulness practices.

Bibliography

Ayuso-Mateos, José Luis, Marta Miret, Francisco Félix Caballero, Beatriz Olaya, Josep Maria Haro, Paul Kowal, and Somnath Chatterji. 'Multi-Country Evaluation of Affective Experience: Validation of an Abbreviated Version of the Day Reconstruction Method in Seven Countries'. *PLOS ONE* 8.4 (2013): 1–8.

Brans, Karen, Iven Van Mechelen, and Bernard Rimé, 'To Share, or Not to Share? Examining the Emotional Consequences of Social Sharing in the Case of Anger and Sadness'. *Emotion* 14.6 (2014): 1062–1071.

Daly, Michael, Roy Baumeister, Liam Delaney, and Malcolm MacLachlan, 'Self-Control and its Relation to Emotions and Psychobiology: Evidence from a Day Reconstruction Method Study'. *Journal of Behavioral Medicine* 37 (2014): 81–93.

Cohen, Sheldon, William J. Doyle, Ronald B. Turner, Cuneyt M. Alper and David P. Skoner. 'Emotional Style and Susceptibility to the Common Cold'. *Psychosomatic Medicine* 65.4 (2003): 652–657.

Dockray, Samantha, Nina Grant, Arthur A. Stone, Daniel Kahneman, Jane Wardle, and Andrew Steptoe. 'A Comparison of Affect Ratings Obtained with Ecological Momentary Assessment and the Day Reconstruction Method'. *Social Indicators Research* 99.2 (2010): 269–283.

Ferrer-i-Carbonell, Ada. 'Income and Well-Being: An Empirical Analysis of the Comparison Income Effect'. *Journal of Public Economics* 89.5–6 (2005): 997–1019.

Frisch, Michael B., Michelle P. Clark, Steven V. Rouse, M. David Rudd, Jennifer K. Paweleck, Andrew Greenston, and David A. Kopplin. 'Predictive and Treatment Validity of Life Satisfaction and the Quality of Life Inventory'. *Assessment* 12 (2005): 66–78.

Kahneman, Daniel, Alan B. Krueger, David A. Schkade, Norbert Schwarz and Arthur A. Stone. 'A Survey Method for Characterizing Daily Life Experience: The Day Reconstruction Method'. *Science* 306.5702 (2004): 1776–1780.

Kahneman, Daniel and Alan B. Krueger. 'Developments in the Measurement of Subjective Well-being'. *Journal of Economic Perspectives* 20 (2006): 3–24.

Nussbaum, Martha. 'Mill between Aristotle and Bentham'. *Economics and Happiness: Framing the Analysis*, edited by Luigino Bruni and Pier Luigi Porta, 170–183. Oxford: Oxford University Press, 2007.

Schwarz, Norbert and Gerald L. Clore. 'Mood, Misattribution, and Judgments of Well – Being: Informative and Directive Functions of Affective States'. *Journal of Personality and Social Psychology* 45.3 (1983): 513–523.

Srivastava, Sanjay, Kimberly M. Angelo, and Shawn R. Vallereux, 'Extraversion and Positive Affect: A Day Reconstruction Study of Person–Environment Transactions'. *Journal of Research in Personality* 42 (2008): 1613:1618.

Urry, Heather, Jack Nitschke, Isa Dolski, Daren Jackson, Kim Dalton, Corrina Mueler, Melissa Rosenkranz, Carol Ryff, Burton Singer, and Richard Davidson. 'Making a Life Worth Living'. *Psychological Science* 15.6 (2004): 367–372.

Waterman, Alan. 'When Effort is Enjoyed: Two Studies of Intrinsic Motivation for Personally Salient Activities'. *Motivation and Emotion* 29 (2005): 165–188.

Wexler, Ellen. 'Should Colleges Measure Well-Being?'. *Inside Higher Ed.* 21 January 2016. Viewed on 21 January 2016. https://www.insidehighered.com/news/2016/01/21/what-colleges-can-do-measure-and-promote-students-well-being.

Zullig, Keith, Eugene Huebner, & Scott Pun. 'Demographic Correlates of Domain-Based Life Satisfaction Reports of College Students'. *Journal of Happiness Studies* 10 (2009): 229–238.

CHAPTER 5

Hegemonic Systems and the Politics of Happiness: the Fairy Tale as Ideology

Sheila M. Rucki and Lisa Ortiz

Abstract

The products of the culture industry, presented as entertainment, are one front in the battle for control and domination. In this paper, we interrogate the notion of happiness presented in the 18th century version of Beauty and the Beast to illustrate how this apparently innocuous children's story carries within it traces of the struggle between an emergent bourgeois class and the nobility to assert cultural, economic and political control. We use the critical insights of Karl Marx and Antonio Gramsci to inform this investigation and make recommendations for future research in later incarnations of this persistent fairy tale.

Keywords

Beauty and the Beast – fairy tales – hegemony – Gramsci – Marx

1   Introduction

At the conclusion of Jeanne-Marie Le Prince de Beaumont's 1756 version of *Beauty and the Beast*, after the Beast has been revealed to be a prince and Beauty has passed the moral test of having 'preferred virtue before wit or beauty' and the two are married, thus elevating Beauty from the merchant class to royalty, the reader is assured that 'their happiness, as it was founded on virtue, was complete.'[1] Astute readers are not surprised by this conclusion. Beyond the traditional fairy tale ending of happily ever after, at each turn in the story Beauty exemplifies the kind

---

1   Marie Le Prince de Beaumont, *Beauty and the Beast: A Tale for the Entertainment of Juvenile Readers*. (1756; Project Gutenberg, 2014), np, viewed 18 January 2016, www.gutenberg.org/files/7074.

of virtue that, we are told, leads to happiness under any circumstances. Her final reward does not make her happy; her happiness leads to the final reward.

As a didactic work intended for juvenile readers, Beaumont's *Beauty and the Beast* is not simply entertaining. It inculcates in the reader a lesson on how to achieve happiness under any circumstances while holding out the promise of a better life, even class mobility, as a reward for adopting the appropriate virtues. These virtues are not subtle and if the reader finds them obscure Beaumont helpfully contrasts them with the unhappy, and quite unpleasant, image of Beauty's sisters.

In this paper, we shall unpack the notion of happiness at work in Beaumont and, using the critical theory insights of Antonio Gramsci, suggest that the persistence of this fairy tale and its underlying theme of happiness through a particular kind of virtue serve as a window into the prevailing ideological imperatives of the historical moment in which it was produced. In this, we take seriously Jack Zipes' admonition that the origins of fairy tales must be located in politics and class struggle.[2] In the end, we argue that understanding the concept of happiness as an incomplete abstraction allows us to fit this fairy tale into the developing hegemony of the bourgeoisie in 18th century France. Happiness in this context is an ideological construction that reinforces emerging systems of production and control while marking a cultural break from the past. As ideology, further research will show that various conceptualizations of happiness embedded in fairy tales maintain their general function, even as they cross historical contexts, and serves as one element in a struggle to assert class hegemony.

2   The Virtue of Beauty

Throughout the text, Beaumont contrasts Beauty with her sisters. Beauty is "better" than her sisters because she is neither prideful nor social. She is kind, loyal, self-sacrificing so self aware that, after her father is driven into poverty by business misfortune, she 'must try to make (herself) happy without a fortune.'[3] In contrast, by the end of the story her sisters have indulged in all seven of the deadly sins and are sentenced to stand as statues at Beauty's palace, where their punishment is to behold her happiness. Given the story to that point, that has been their sad fate all along; their magical transformation into statues

---

2   Jack Zipes, 'Breaking the Magic Spell: Politics and the Fairy Tale,' *New German Critique*, 6 (Autumn 1975): 118, viewed 18 January 2016, http://www.jstore.org/stable/487657.
3   Beaumont, *Beauty and the Beast.*

is unnecessary in that they have been forced to stand witness to Beauty's happiness from the beginning.

This story of happiness must be set in its historical context. *Beauty and the Beast* comes to us as a literary text as part of the great wave of the 18th and 19th century transformation of oral folk traditions into texts intended for literate audiences.[4] As described by Zipes in several of his works, this transformation of form and audience removes much of the original utopian content of the folk tradition, wherein common people recognize and resist their oppressors *via* magical interventions or violence, and replaces it with didactic messages focused on proper behaviour and the development of bourgeois morality.[5] It also emerges at a moment when the nobility of France is in rapid demographic and cultural decline under pressures from both its internal contradictions and the advances of a capitalist class embedded in international trade and rapid urbanization.[6]

Beauty and the Beast is also atypical in the way it ascribes class status throughout. Beauty and her family are not rural peasants confronting oppression in the form of force from economic and political superiors, starvation or stepmothers. They are an upwardly mobile merchant family. The father (there is no mother) is introduced as having once been wealthy and sparing no expense for his children's education. They are part of an urban elite driven to rural life by commercial setback. Here Beaumont goes to some length to describe the impact of this fall. Venal suitors for the sisters evaporate with the wealth, the sons become farmers and Beauty takes on the burdens of housekeeping. Even in this reduced condition the merchant continues to participate in the import of goods, he first encounters the Beast in an attempt to reclaim goods recently arrived from abroad, and apparently retained some house staff in that when Beauty returns to her father's house she is first encountered by a maid who, upon seeing Beauty, gives out a loud shriek.[7] So while they are relatively impoverished they never lose the behavioural or hierarchical attributes of their class status. Finally, Beauty's reward for her virtue is to transcend her class status and enter into the nobility with her marriage to the Beast.

This story, then, is a story intended for a literate bourgeois audience and provides instruction for class mobility, rooted in the full personification of

---

4   Jack Zipes, *Breaking the Magic Spell: Radical Theories of Folk and Fairy Tales, Revised and Expanded Edition* (Lexington, Kentucky: University Press of Kentucky, 1979), 10.
5   Zipes, *Breaking the Magic Spell*, 7–11.
6   William Doyle, *Aristocracy and its Enemies in the Age of Revolution* (Oxford: Oxford University Press, 2009), 9–36.
7   Beaumont, *Beauty and the Beast*.

bourgeois virtue. Beauty does not need to deploy magic or deceit to enjoy class mobility. Rather, a strict adherence to bourgeois virtues allows her to break the magical spell that had impeded her rise. Merchants rise above their class not by the use of force, outwitting, or deploying magic against their oppressors but by working hard and mastering the virtues of their class.

3   Happiness as an Incomplete Abstraction

In the 1756 version of Beauty and the Beast, happiness is presented in a way that harkens back to the work of Aristotle. In particular, happiness is a result of flourishing (*eudaimonia*) or functioning well according to one's nature. In the context of 18th century bourgeois France, this takes the form of Beauty's virtue, which allows her to flourish in each of her economic contexts: wealthy urban elite, rural housemistress, self-sacrificing captive of the Beast and queen. Of course, this is only one way of understanding happiness. If we begin with this formulation, however, we can begin to construct a mechanism for understanding the role of happiness in an ideological context. More specifically, this is a starting point for uncovering how the concept of happiness functions didactically to reinforce existing relations production and domination within the context of hegemonic control. What does this particular formulation of happiness tell us about the developing hegemony of the emergent 18th century bourgeoisie?

A   *Antonio Gramsci and the Theory of Hegemony*

For Gramsci, effective systems of control are understood as hegemonic. Under these conditions, interlocking and reinforcing systems of economic and cultural production facilitate the domination of subordinate economic actors by extracting their willing consent.[8] Consent is the product of a common, unifying, culture that universalizes the particular interest of the dominant class and creates a unified subjective class-consciousness that obscures the reality of class conflict.[9] Cultural production, even in the form of the literary fairy tale, is a class project that normalizes its cultural and economic interests while marginalizing or casting as deviant those of others. Under hegemonic conditions,

---

[8] Stephen Gill and David Law, 'Global hegemony and the structural power of capital,' *Gramsci, Historical Materialism, and International Relations,* ed. Stephen Gill (Cambridge: Cambridge University Press, 1993), 93.

[9] Antonio Gramsci, *Selections from the Prison Notebooks,* trans. and ed. Quintin Hoare and Geoffrey Nowell Smith (New York: International Publishers, 1971), 181.

these class-specific productions present themselves as universal, both reflecting and being reinforced by the coercive power of the state and modes of production. Together, they generate consensual orders that are relatively stable and from within which individual actors understand themselves. Resistance is minimized and any that does emerge is relegated to expression through the contradictions inevitably created by the hegemonic system itself. The unifying product of cultural production, the particular disguised as the universal, is the critical content of ideology.

In this framework, the literary fairy tale can be understood as an element in the production of ideology, aimed at a particular economic class, and containing within it notions of self and identity that tend to reinforce prevailing modes of production. However, even though systems of economic and cultural production are intertwined in this framework, they are not identical. Each emerges from an historical context, adapted to a particular historical moment. To use another Gramscian term, the literary fairy tale carries with it the "common sense", meaning the sensibilities and world views of common folks, of its prior oral folk tradition even as that tradition is adapted to a new audience and to a new function of compliance rather than resistance. Thus, the challenge of a political-economic reading of fairy tales is to unwind the vestigial imagery and motifs (magical transformations of beasts, medieval forests, the power of utterances) from its didactic message of compliance in its historical context (virtues of hard work, loyalty and self-sacrifice). The incomplete abstraction of the concept of happiness provides the opportunity for this unwinding.

B   *Dialectical Abstraction and Beauty's Happiness*
To grasp the role of happiness in *Beauty and the Beast*, it is first necessary to place the concept into a dialectical framework. Karl Marx models this process through what he refers to as abstraction. For Marx, the process of abstraction is how we move from "real concrete", that is the world as it presents itself experientially, to the "thought concrete"; the reconstitution of the whole as mental constructs that can be manipulated and reconfigured in relation to each other, creating a mental representation of reality that is both partial and comprehendible. This transformation is performed through abstraction, wherein the experiential world is broken into discrete and simplified mental units, concepts, that have spatial and temporal boundaries and can be thought about independently.[10] However, concepts, be they as apparently material as money

---

10   Bertell Ollman, *The Dance of the Dialectic: Steps in Marx's Method* (Chicago: University of Illinois Press, 2003), 60.

or as ephemeral as happiness, cannot be usefully thought of as things unto themselves, even if they must be initially reduced to such as part of our mental processes. No thing, in Marx's dialectic, can be considered separate from the relations it entails. Focusing on one relation and then another provides multiple perspectives or vantage points, which further expands the universe of relations and includes the past, present and future of those concepts. Thus, in one of Marx's more famous examples, labour power and commodities, which appear as distinct concepts, are only different vantage points in the same relations. Understanding this leads to a useful conceptualization not only of what labour is but what it is in the process of becoming.[11]

Consistent with Gramsci, ideology is the product of an incomplete abstraction, which is to see a relation from a single vantage point that obscures the actual multiplicity of relations in favour of the interests of a dominant class perspective. Incomplete abstractions are ultimately ill fitting in that they do not express a sufficient array of vantage points that comprise the concept. They are hegemonic insofar as they obscure or denigrate relations that do not tend to support the political and economic structures beneficial to the dominant class. Beginning with the premise that the conceptualization of happiness entailed in *Beauty and the Beast* can be understood not as a condition of virtue but as a set of relations between Beauty and the other characters of the story, unpacking those relations exposes the emergent 18th century bourgeoisie and provides a template of behaviour that moulds its members into "productive" members of that class while promising that those who resist will be punished. In this concept of happiness we find clues to the hegemonic ideology that is both its source and its product.

4 Controls, Ideology and the Concept of Happiness

The construct of happiness in Beaumont's *Beauty and the Beast* reads as a litany of behaviours necessary for the successful performance of bourgeois identity. In contrast to her sisters, Beauty is indifferent to opulent consumption and frivolity, inclined to hard work and industrious behaviour and is willing to sacrifice herself for others. Even in her decision to marry the Beast, she is driven not by courtly love but by 'gratitude, esteem and friendship.'[12] She does

---

11 Karl Marx, *Capital: Volume One,* trans. Ben Fowkes (New York: Vintage Books, 1977), Part 2, Ch. 6.
12 Beaumont, *Beauty and the Beast*, 9.

not long for a romantic connection but rather a kind of a satisfying business relationship. However, this reading rests on an incomplete abstraction. The virtues of the bourgeoisie are seen only from the vantage point of the bourgeoisie. By expanding the abstraction, we get hints of suppressed resistance. How does Beauty's happiness look from the perspective of her sisters? On this, Beaumont is not a reliable narrator. If Beauty's happiness is to have its edifying effect, her sisters must be unhappy. The relations on which this unhappiness rests are the virtues of courtly life. A quick and ready wit, gaiety, displays of opulence, and a desire for romantic marriages of beauty and charm are all sources of unhappiness even as they reflect the virtues of the old order. Imagining Beauty from her sisters' perspective, however, is illuminating. From birth, we are told, that Beauty was her father's favourite. The sisters' attempts to enjoy class mobility by marrying into the nobility are derided and when they continue to perform the virtues of the noble class after the fortune is lost they are only held in contempt. From their perspective, Beauty must seem to be flaunting social expectations. She does not cultivate the virtues of wit and charm, she does not take advantage of opportunities for class mobility, and she does not conform to the expectations of courtly behaviour or dress. And yet she is the favourite. From the perspective of her sisters, Beauty's happiness must be mystifying; she is rewarded for what can appear to them only as a wilful rejection of the prevailing social standards.

If we re-imagine Beauty's happiness from her father's perspective, we see yet another facet of emergent capitalism as a hegemonic system. The father's primary motive throughout the story is to provide for his family. He leaves the countryside to conduct business in a failed attempt to reverse his fortunes. He angers the Beast by first taking advantage of his hospitality and then cutting a rose to take home to Beauty. He even resists Beauty's decision to surrender to the Beast in order to spare his life.[13] Throughout he is motivated by fealty to his nuclear family, defined by his role as provider and attaches whatever happiness he enjoys to the successful performance of that role.

Finally, Beauty's happiness must also be envisioned from the vantage point of the Beast. Throughout much of the story, the Beast is a morose character who seems to miss the point of bourgeois happiness in his insistence that while she is his captive she avail herself of the luxuries of his palace. Although we do not know it, he is the victim of a wicked fairy whose only avenue to happiness is to win Beauty's loyalty and assimilate those virtues to himself through marriage.

---

13   It should be said that from our perspective he is swayed to let Beauty surrender a little too easily by Beauty's dream.

By the rules of the curse that forces him to appear as the Beast, he may not use his courtly charms to win Beauty's hand. Thus, even though he is both handsome and witty, he presents himself to Beauty as ugly, having no sense and a 'poor, silly, stupid creature.'[14] To him, Beauty's happiness must seem a kind of redemption, but redemption that he is wholly incapable of effecting on his own. As he tells Beauty 'only you in the world [is] generous enough to be won by the goodness of my temper.'[15] His wealth and title are not sources of happiness, nor can he use them to achieve happiness. It is clear that he can be happy only when Beauty joins with him. When he fears she is lost to him he nearly expires. Thus, from the vantage point of nobility, happiness, perhaps even survival, is possible only by assuming the bourgeois virtues of the emergent merchant class and that class must be seduced into sharing those virtues. *Beauty and the Beast*, then, completes the triumph of bourgeois ideology; happiness obtains only for those who adopt the values and virtues of the bourgeoisie. Upon their marriage, Beauty supplants the ideology of the old order with that of the new with the willing consent of the order she is replacing.

5 Conclusion

Shorn of its magic and the remnants of the oral tradition from which it sprang, *Beauty and the Beast* is a children's primer into the willing acquiescence to a hegemonic system of asserting control in the liminal space between feudalism and capitalism. Beyond that, it articulates an ideological position that not only explains the decline of pre-capitalist systems but predicts that the remnants of that class must adopt the virtues of the insurgent class if it is to survive at all. In the best Marxist tradition, the concept of happiness illuminates not only what marks bourgeois hegemony but also what it is becoming.

The extent to which this reading is useful can be tested by analysing subsequent versions of happiness in later versions of *Beauty and the Beast*.

Bibliography

de Beaumont, Marie Le Prince. *Beauty and the Beast: A Tale for the Entertainments of Juvenile Readers*. Project Gutenberg, 2014. Viewed 18 January 2016-04-12 2016. www.gutenberg.org/files/7074.

---

14   Beaumont, *Beauty and the Beast*, 6.
15   Beaumont, *Beauty and the Beast*, 8.

Doyle, William. *Aristocracy and its Enemies in the Age of Revolution.* Oxford: Oxford University Press, 2009.

Gill, Stephen and David Law. 'Global hegemony and the structural power of capital.' *Gramsci, Historical Materialism, and International Relations,* edited by Stephen Gill, 93–125. Cambridge: Cambridge University Press, 1993.

Gramsci, Antonio. *Selections from the Prison Notebooks.* Translated and edited by Quintin Hoare and Geoffrey Nowell Smith. New York: International Publishers, 1971.

Marx, Karl. *Capital: Volume One.* Translated by Ben Fowkes. New York: Vintage Books, 1977.

Ollman, Bertell. *The Dance of the Dialectic: Steps in Marx's Method.* Chicago: University of Illinois Press, 2003.

Zipes, Jack. 'Breaking the Magic Spell: Politics and the Fairy Tale.' *New German Critique*, 6 (Autumn 1975): 116–135. Viewed 18 January 2016. http://www.jstore.org/stable/487657.

Zipes, Jack. *Breaking the Magic Spell: Radical Theories of Folk and Fairy Tales, Revised and Expanded Edition.* Lexington, Kentucky: University of Kentucky Press, 2003.

CHAPTER 6

Using Art Therapy Techniques to Explore Home Life Happiness

Emily Corrigan-Kavanagh, Carolina Escobar-Tello and Kathy Pui Ying Lo

Abstract

The home plays many roles in our daily lives. It provides shelter and a place to rest. It can be viewed as an extension of the self, portraying our hopes and ideals. However, contemporary homes are filled with modern appliances that tend to offer few opportunities for creative output or experience by placing an emphasis on productivity, reducing potential for self-reflection and psychological growth. This lifestyle of high consumption does not necessarily correlate with long-term happiness but there's evidence to suggest engagement in creativity can. Furthermore, art creation can engage the emotional centres of the brain and potentially be used to investigate and enhance home happiness. In particular, art therapy techniques (for example, art making in silence) can be used to trigger and explore positive emotions, as this paper will illustrate. Based in the UK, this research will therefore explore how creativity can contribute to home by using approaches from art therapy. A series of workshops, comprising family homeowners, guided by the researcher, used techniques from this field to investigate how home happiness might be developed/facilitated. This paper will present the findings from this, such as creating the right context for reflective art making and facilitating emotional expression with a focus on positive family time.

Keywords

creativity – happiness – home – art therapy techniques – emotions – flow – positive family experiences

1   Introduction

According to Nakamura and Csikszentmihalyi, a happy life is one that contains moments of flow – the complete absorption in what one does, using personal strengths to master challenges.[1] Art making has been documented in art therapy to encourage experiences of flow.[2] Furthermore, it has been shown by research using fMRI scans, to provide alternative access to emotional centers in the brain when emotional mood drawings are created as this appears to activate corresponding neurological areas.[3] This suggests that art therapy techniques can be used to elicit positive emotional responses and explore happiness. In this research, they were used to investigate positive experiences in the home.

1.1 The Creative and Influential Home

The human need for self-expression can clearly be witnessed in the home. 'The showcase of the self' refers to the human tendency to gather, arrange and display artefacts of emotional and social relevance in this space to develop a personal representation within a particular social context.[4] Home is 'a shelter for those things that make life meaningful',[5] a reminder of those attributes we respect and those we feel we are lacking.[6] Accordingly, it is an evolving space,[7] full of dialectic practices between individuals, objects and society.[8]

Homes in this manner can influence our behaviour. For example, it can encourage social interaction by providing inviting communal spaces. Furthermore, our daily habits can influence up to 40% of our experienced happiness.[9] Homes, by enabling certain activities or not, can affect our happiness.

---

1 Jeanne Nakamura and Mihalyi Csikszentmihalyi, 'The Concept of Flow', *Handbook of Positive Psychology*, ed. Charles R. Snyder and Shane J. Lopez (Oxford: Oxford Univeristy Press, 2002), 89–105.
2 Amy Voytilla, 'Flow states during art making' (MA diss., The School of the Art Institute of Chicago, 2006).
3 Vija B. Lusebrink and Palo Alto, 'Art Therapy and the Brain: An Attempt to Understand the Underlying Processes of Art Expression in Therapy', 125–135.
4 Cristoforetti, Gennai and Rodeschini, 'Home sweet home: The emotional construction of places', 225–232.
5 Mihalyi Csikszentmihalyi and Eugene Rochberg-Halton, *The Meaning of Things: Domestic Symbols and the Self* (Cambridge: Cambridge University Press, 1981), 139.
6 Alain De Botton, *The Architecture Of Happiness*.
7 Kimberly Dovey, 'Home and Homelessness: Introduction', *Home Environments. Human Behavior and Environment: Advances in Theory and Research*, eds. Irwin Altman and Carol M. Werner (New York: Plenum Press, 1985), 33–64.
8 Tim Ingold, *Being Alive: Essays on Movement, Knowledge and Description* (London: New York: Routledge, 2011).
9 Sonja Lyubomirsky, Kennon M. Sheldon and David Schkade, 'Pursuing Happiness: The Architecture of Sustainable Change', *Review of General Psychology* 9.2 (2005): 111–131.

1.2 *Contemporary Domestic Lifestyles*

However, contemporary consumerist lifestyles have resulted in many homes filled with commercial design products and appliances that discourage positive engagement. This is because most of modern design offers few opportunities for creativity[10] and instead, arguably, focus on satisfying biological needs for *pleasure*. Csikszentmihalyi[15] characterises *pleasure* as the harmonious feeling resulting from a physiological need (for example, sleep) being met. However, solely fulfilling pleasure needs in the home cannot bring happiness as this subsequently creates contexts of productivity and evanescence that lack emotional complexity. Life must also have experiences of *enjoyment*, those that contain novelty, a sense of accomplishment (i.e. the development of a new skill) and instances of *flow*.[11] Evidently, current lifestyles of high consumption do not necessarily correlate with long-term happiness and have been linked to higher levels of depression.[12]

1.3 *Happiness in the Home*

Notably, research has shown that the existence of strong social relationships can lead to higher levels of reported happiness[13] and these could be facilitated in the home. Findings from the previous study[14] of this research supported this in which photo elicitation was used as a combined interview and creative method. 13 participants from home-owning families created photographic narratives of their domestic routines, later discussing these in semi-structured interviews. This caused them to deeply reflect about happiness triggers in the home and revealed several needs for home life happiness. The most prominent of these needs were self-love, reciprocal love and companionship in which positive time spent with family (for example, relaxing together) appeared to

---

10   Elizabeth Sanders and Pieter Jan Stappers, 'Co-creation and the new landscapes of design', *CoDesign* 4.March (2008): 5–18.

11   Mihalyi Csikszentmihalyi, *Flow: The Psychology of Happiness: The Classic Work on How to Achieve Happiness*, 46.

12   Patrick Hofstetter, Michael Madjar and Toshisuke Ozawa, 'Happiness and Sustainable Consumption: Psychological and physical rebound effects at work in a tool for sustainable design Patrick', 105–115. Ed Diener and Martine Seligman, 'Beyond Money: Towards an Economy of Wellbeing', *American Psychology Society* 5.1 (2004): 1–31.

13   Ed Diener and Martin Seligman, 'Very Happy People', *American Psychology Society* 13.1 (2002): 81–84.

14   Emily Corrigan-Doyle, Carolina Escobar-Tello and Kathy Pui Ying Lo, 'Taking a Softer Approach: Using Photo Elicitation to Explore the Home as a System for Happiness and Sustainability' (paper presented at 20th Sustainable Innovation conference, UCA, Surrey, November 9–10, 2015).

satisfy these needs simultaneously. It was therefore decided to continue to use image making (i.e. art therapy techniques) to explore the happiness aspects of positive time with family in greater detail through a series of workshops. This paper will present findings from the first of these workshops.

2 Using Art Therapy Techniques to Explore Happiness in the Home

Art therapy is a type of psychotherapy that uses art creation to treat physiological and mental disorders or to aid in self-development.[15] In this, techniques such as silence and spontaneous art making can be used to help participants visualise feelings and thoughts that are difficult to verbalise[16] and outsider interpretation of resulting artefacts is mostly discouraged[17] to promote emotional authenticity.[18]

This workshop tested the appropriateness of art therapy techniques for the exploration of positive family time. Given their usual therapeutic setting, it was essential to trial these creative techniques in a preliminary study so that the most appropriate could be identified, modified if necessary and brought forward in later workshops.

2.1 *Participants*

This was a pilot study to test the viability of art therapy techniques to explore home life happiness. Furthermore, it is recommended for the numbers in a group art therapy session to be kept low (between 6 and 12) to afford each individual adequate attention,[19] so the group was intentionally kept small. Participants in this pilot study consisted of two male and two female, aged between 27 and 55 from different disciplinary backgrounds.

---

15   Cathy Malchiodi, *The Art Therapy Sourcebook 2nd Edition* (Hove: New York: Bruner-Routledge, 2007).
16   Cathy Malchiodi, *The Art Therapy Sourcebook 2nd Edition*. Cathy Malchiodi, *The Handbook of Art Therapy* (New York: The Guilford Press 2003). Judith A. Rubin, *The Art of Art Therapy: What Every Art Therapist Needs to Know* (Routledge: New York: East Sussex, 2011).
17   Liesl Silverstone, *Art Therapy Exercises: Inspirational and Practical Ideas to Stimulate the Imagination* (London: Jessica Kingsley Publishers, 2009). Cathy Malchiodi, *The Art Therapy Sourcebook 2nd Edition*. Judith A. Rubin, *The Art of Art Therapy: What Every Art Therapist Needs to Know*.
18   Judith A. Rubin, *The Art of Art Therapy: What Every Art Therapist Needs to Know*.
19   Marian Liebmann, *Art Therapy for Groups: A handbook of themes and exercises* (Hove: New York: Bruner-Routledge, 2004).

2.2 Procedure

This preliminary workshop was performed at an appropriate venue for art therapy techniques. The room was close to a sink (for washing brushes and hands), it had large windows (for natural light), and had ample table space and areas to work on and hang art.[20] The workshop was planned to last a total of 1.5 hours and was divided into three tasks. The activities and their purpose are summarised in order of occurrence in the table 6.1.

The workshop facilitator used the 'participant observation' approach and took on the role of 'participant-as-observer'.[21] Instructions for activities were narrated to participants and were also demonstrated (i.e. through pictorial examples) to help participants understand the workshop's expectations.

At the end of the workshop, participants completed a feedback form and unstructured interviews[22] were carried out to clarify their initial thoughts about the session. Due to the reflective nature of the workshop it was deemed important to allow participants additional time to consider their experiences. To that end, one-to-one semi-structured interviews[23] were carried out with participants a few days after the workshop.

2.3 Analysis Strategy

The workshop and interviews' data (video, audio footage, field notes) was analysed for evidence of deep reflection around home happiness. This was done using analytical memos, session summary sheets[24] and sensitising questions.[25]

Full transcriptions were created from the audio recordings of the workshop and semi-structured interviews in order to sensitise the investigator to responses that illustrated relevant deep reflection. Analytical memos were utilised to clarify overall impressions after the workshop sessions and semi-structured interviews. Sensitising questions (i.e. How is this scenario encouraging reflection about positive family time?) were then used to amplify important aspects that indicated reflection in participants such as facial expressions of intense contemplation.

---

20   Cathy Malchiodi, *The Art Therapy Sourcebook 2nd Edition*.
21   Colin Robson, *Real World Research: A Resource for Social Scientists and Practitioner – Researchers 3rd Edition* (Oxford: Blackwell Publishers ltd, 2011).
22   Ibid.
23   Ibid.
24   Juliet Corbin and Anselm L. Strauss. *Basics of Qualitative Research: Techniques and Tools for Developing Grounded Theory* (Thousand Oaks: SAGE Publications, 2008), 247–263.
25   Colin Robson, *Real World Research: A Resource for Social Scientists and Practitioner – Researchers 3rd Edition*.

TABLE 6.1 Tasks and procedures followed in workshop and rationales

Task	Procedure	Rationale
Activity 1. Image awareness exercise	Prior to the workshop, participants were asked to pick an area in their homes where they spent the most time and carefully observe the imagery around them, making reflective notes and/or drawings on what they liked or didn't like, would like more of or would like to change. For the first activity of the workshop participants were asked to share their outcomes with the group.	This was applied to establish initial interest before the workshop and to make participants more aware of significant images they kept in their personal spaces. In this manner, it was to help them draw meaning from later resulting artworks because the unconscious mind is influenced by images and this can influence the artwork that one creates.[a] Furthermore, asking participants to share these outcomes at the workshop was used as an icebreaker activity.
Activity 2. Spontaneous art making	Participants were given a black outline of a house as a template to decorate the page using any of the materials available without speaking. Once this time was up, they were each requested to explain the image they had created to the rest of the group.	This spontaneous art making technique was used to allow participants to visually free associate what home meant to them. Discussing their imagery with the group afterwards was used to assist participants in initially reflecting and understanding the meaning of their artefact.[b] It was also to encourage collective learning[c] as these overt contemplations might serve to trigger insights for other participants about the significance of their own artwork

TABLE 6.1 (*cont.*)

Task	Procedure	Rationale
Activity 3. Visualising positive family time	Participants were asked to visualise a positive experience with family members using any of the materials provided, again without speaking. Lastly, they were asked to individually discuss their images i.e. what it represented and reasons for their chosen colours, shapes, sizes and forms.	Having become more sensitised visually and emotionally to their personal understanding of home from previous exercises, this session was used to focus participants' attention on the concept of positive family time.

[a] Mihalyi Csikszentmihalyi, *Flow: The Psychology of Happiness: The Classic Work on How to Achieve Happiness*.
[b] Ibid.
[c] Marian Liebmann, *Art Therapy for Groups: A Handbook of Themes, Games and Exercises* (New York: Routledge, 1986).

3 Results and Discussion

The analysis of the results identified applicable techniques that facilitated participants' deep reflection and expression of feelings, both visually and verbally, to take forward in subsequent workshops. The ability of art therapy techniques to induce positive affect and generate insights around positive family time was also indicated. These findings will be discussed in detail in the following sections.

3.1 *Creating the Right Context for Reflective Art Making*

Activity 1 discussions suggested that the preparatory image awareness exercise triggered participants' interest in the workshop prior to the session. It seemed to stimulate reflection about their aesthetical preferences for visuals in their surroundings and the significance of this (i.e. how these enforced or could facilitate their happiness). For example, one participant observed after doing this exercise that his current home environment felt more like an office space as his main living area was quite bare. In this, he remarked that he would like to change 'the office shelves' for a 'more homely oval' bookcase

FIGURE 6.1   Read from left to right, image showing notes and drawings from the activity 1 (image awareness exercise), then artwork from activity 2 (spontaneous art making) and activity 3 (visualising positive family time).
ORIGINAL ARTWORK CREATED BY PARTICIPANTS. PHOTOGRAPHED BY RESEARCHER. USED WITH PERMISSION.

because otherwise 'you just feel like you're at work … 24 hours a day'. It thus appeared to create the right context for later artistic expression aimed at illustrating feelings (i.e. the happiness aspects of positive family time) as oppose to rational thoughts. Furthermore, as they were given the freedom to illustrate their results through writing or imagery – with two out of four participants using both – it encouraged participants to start thinking about their feelings visually.

Additionally, the use of spontaneous image making in activity 2 appeared to serve as an adequate warm-up exercise towards art making. It allowed participants to select and experiment with any medium of their choosing to create randomised imagery. Participants were initially timid in approaching the materials but their confidence appeared to improve over time. For example, by activity 3 all participants had transitioned from just using one form of medium (i.e. colouring pencils) to using many simultaneously (i.e. coloured paper, crayons, glue) (see Figure 6.1).

However, as different materials were placed at different points of the table where the participants were seated, this appeared to influence their material choices. For example, piles of magazines placed at the end of the table were left untouched for the duration of the workshop. Accordingly, materials could be evenly dispersed within easy reach of participants in future workshops to limit this.

Nonetheless, the resulting artwork was very personal to each individual and, consequentially, incoherent to the facilitator without additional explanations.

FIGURE 6.2   A montage of all artwork created during the Happy Homes Workshop.
ORIGINAL ARTWORK CREATED BY PARTICIPANTS. PHOTOGRAPHED BY
RESEARCHER. USED WITH PERMISSION.

This provided a safeguard against making personal evaluations of the artwork and dismissing participants' feedback. Collectively, the techniques appeared to emphasise participants' individuality i.e. how they thought of the world differently (see Figure 6.2).

3.2   *Inducing Experiences of 'Flow'*

Evidently, by providing participants with a variety of materials to use and gradually advancing the tasks, participants appeared to experience periods of *flow*[30] during the session. For instance, as the preparatory activity allowed them to document their thoughts through illustration or writing and activities 2 and 3 allowed freedom of material use, participants could engage in the tasks at their own level and pace, advancing their activity when ready.

Furthermore, all participants stated that conducting the art making in silence (activity 2 and 3) greatly aided in their concentration and immersion in the tasks. They asserted that discussions might have influenced the content of the resulting imagery. Observing participants silently working on artwork during the workshop and subsequently using the recorded video footage further confirmed this. Participants appeared to be heavily engaged in the tasks – their gestures and body language (i.e. contemplative expressions and pauses followed by meditated actions) indicated that they were carefully selecting materials and making thoughtful decisions about their compositions. Subsequently, all resulting artworks were very unique and different when compared collectively (see Figure 6.3).

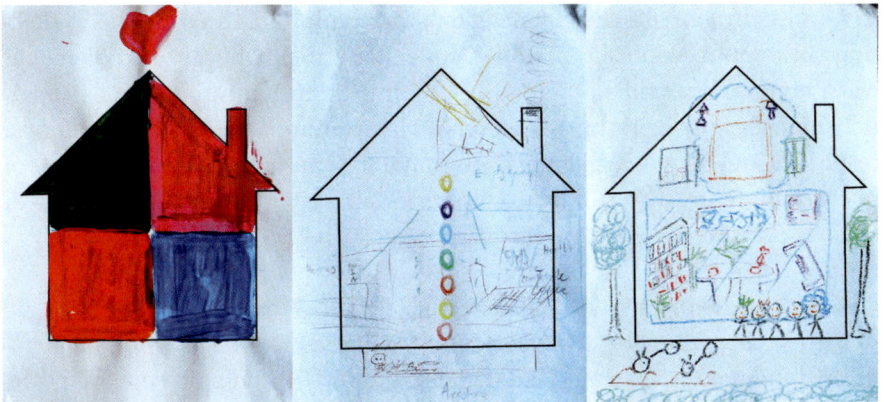

FIGURE 6.3   A selection of images created during activity 2 (spontaneous art making).
ORIGINAL ARTWORK CREATED BY PARTICIPANTS. PHOTOGRAPHED BY RESEARCHER. USED WITH PERMISSION.

3.3   *Facilitating Emotional Expression*

The image awareness exercise appeared to trigger appropriate responses in participants (i.e. descriptions of how they *felt* as opposed to what they thought of their surroundings) prior to the workshop, engaging them emotionally about their visual preferences. The periods when talking was permitted (end of activity 2 and 3) appeared to give participants a platform in which they could share their insights with the rest of the group while limiting distraction from the art making process itself and rationalising of imagery. By requiring participants to immediately discuss their artwork or listen to others speak about theirs, they were forced to express or hold onto their initial reactions before these became distorted by conscious reconsideration. This was made evident by three out of four participants overtly reassessing what they were saying while they were explaining their image to the group. Such comments included, 'I have somehow managed to dismiss my entire family' and 'They're like chakras … maybe half of them should be missing'.

Additionally, throughout the workshop the facilitator maintained a neutral composure with participants, not offering any interpretations about images while using eye contact and head nods to assume an attentive stance. As with similar interview techniques (i.e. neutral questioning),[26] this enabled participants to express their thoughts without interruption and, consequently, aided in the creation of a suitable context for open reflection.

---

26   Ibid.

Admittedly, not all participants would be comfortable sharing their reflections in a group scenario or would understand their imagery completely. It was therefore deemed suitable to hold semi-structured interviews with participants after the workshop to accommodate a more private space for honest responses and allow participants additional time to reflect. Further review of relevant literature also confirmed this as a viable approach as the meaning of the artwork could change for participants over time.[27]

3.4 Art Making with a Positive Focus – Positive Family Time

Activity 3 seemed to be effective in enabling participants to be emotionally reflective about positive family time. For example, one participant remarked, 'The best type of memories I have with family are talking about your problems' and another described, 'There's my family with the bottle [of wine] and that's how I picture the summer'. Evidently, because they had to dictate all elements of the image, each participant needed to carefully consider all aesthetical choices in relation to what they were trying to portray. Consequently, this appeared to encourage some to think carefully about the roles each family member played in positive family experiences. For instance, one participant explained why each person was a specific colour and were placed at certain points on the page:

> These are my sisters who are identical twins. That's why they're the same colour and this sort of grey box down here is my mother ... doesn't really fit into what was a tight nit group ... [partner] and I are under here because we do hold the whole group together.

Naturally, some participants were more reflective than others and were better able to give detailed accounts of positive family experiences. Nonetheless, it was clear that all reported experiences shared two qualities; they facilitated the expression of family members' strengths and encouraged experiences of *flow*.[28] For example, one participant described a rewarding weekend where she had to look after her nephews because she is 'the responsible one' who entertains the children. Although the experience was tiring, being with them made her 'feel whole'. Evidently, asking participants to focus on and visualise a positive family experience appear to amplify their momentary happiness by affirming the presence of this in their life. During the follow-up unstructured interviews,

---

27 Cathy Malchiodi, *The Art Therapy Sourcebook 2nd Edition*. Cathy Malchiodi, *The Handbook of Art Therapy*.

28 Mihalyi Csikszentmihalyi, *Flow: The Psychology of Happiness: The Classic Work on How to Achieve Happiness*.

all participants reported that they felt very positive from the experience and wished for it to last longer. In this manner, the workshop also appeared to facilitate a platform for acknowledging the good things in one's home life. Accordingly, this positive affect could encourage greater responsiveness from participants in follow-up semi-structured interviews in subsequent workshops.

4 Conclusions

This workshop provided an enjoyable experience for participants while reaffirming positive aspects of home life. The art making afforded an expressive communication tool for individuals to illustrate their unique thoughts and desires around similar topics at their own pace and level. The image awareness exercise was effective in generating initial interest about the workshop activities. It engaged participants in the visual aspects of their surroundings and its impact on their happiness i.e. the need for separation between work and home.

Activity 2 (spontaneous art making) gave participants a chance to practice with the materials and proved useful in eliciting relevant responses around home, for example, what it meant to them. After conducting these tasks, participants were sensitised to personally significant domestic imagery – by first being made aware of meaningful imagery in their everyday life (i.e. image awareness exercise) and then specifically those related to home (i.e. spontaneous art making activity).

Activity 3 (visualising positive family time) allowed them to focus on positive experiences with family members and illustrate these. Collectively, the three workshop activities (i.e. activity 1, 2 and 3) combined to allow participants a gradual transition from familiar materials (i.e. pencil) to those that were more adventurous (i.e. collage). Furthermore, conducting these activities in silence enabled participants to concentrate on tasks, minimising influence from others. This resulted in all artworks being very personal in appearance, necessitating accompanying comments from participants to clarify meaning. This would therefore reduce the risk of personal biases influencing findings in later workshops. However, it was also noted that participants might not feel comfortable discussing reflections in a group and the meaning of the artwork might change over time. Subsequent sessions would hence include follow-up semi-structured interviews a week after the workshop.

Nonetheless, the resulting images appeared to ease this process as they provided participants with reference points for discussions when sharing insights with the group. Furthermore, as all elements of the image where dictated by the individual, each needed to consider their aesthetical choices, especially when explaining this to the group. This also encouraged individuals to think about the roles each family member played and the events that lead to positive experiences with them. This evidently lead to the preliminary identification of possible conditions for positive family experiences i.e. utilisation of one's strengths and experiences of *flow*[30], that could be further explored in subsequent workshops with semi-structured interviews. Having been sensitised to their personal happiness triggers around positive family time during the workshop, participants would be in a stronger position to deliver insightful answers around these topics. Relevant questions for each participant based on their workshop responses could also be formulated to explore how time with family using one's strengths or experiencing *flow*[30] might be facilitated within the home. Following this process, art therapy techniques could potentially make a valuable contribution to the understanding of happiness in the home.

5 Future Work

This preliminary study confirmed the effectiveness of art therapy techniques in promoting personal emotional connection and demonstrated strong potential in investigating positive family time in the home. The next stages of this research will use these techniques in the second study workshops to explore the concept of positive family time intensely i.e. how the expression of personal strengths and experiences of *flow*[29] are facilitated in these instances. Subsequently, these results will be used will be used by designers in a final workshop to create design interventions (i.e. services) for the facilitation of happy experiences in the home.

Bibliography

Corbin, Juliet and Anselm L. Strauss. *Basics of Qualitative Research 3rd Edition*. Thousand Oaks: SAGE Publications, 2008.

Corrigan-Doyle, Emily, Carolina Escobar-Tello and Kathy Pui Ying Lo. 'Taking a Softer Approach: Using Photo Elicitation to Explore the Home as a System for Happiness and Sustainability'. Paper presented at 20th Sustainable Innovation, UCA, Surrey, November 9–10, 2015.

Cristoforetti, Antonio, Francesca Gennai and Guilia Rodeschini. 'Home Sweet Home: The Emotional Construction of Places'. *Journal of Aging Studies* 25.3 (2011): 225–232.

---

[29] Ibid.

Csikszentmihalyi, Mihalyi and Eugene Rochberg-Halton. *The Meaning of Things: Domestic Symbols and the Self.* Cambridge: Cambridge University Press, 1981, 139.

Csikszentmihalyi, Mihalyi. *Flow: The Psychology of Happiness: The Classic Work on How to Achieve Happiness.* USA: Harper & Row, 2002.

De Botton, Alain. *The Architecture of Happiness.* London: Penguin Group, 2006.

Diener, Ed. and Martin E.P. Seligman. 'Beyond Money: Towards an Economy of Wellbeing'. *American Psychology Society* 5.1 (2004): 1–31

Diener, Ed. and Martin E.P. Seligman. 'Very Happy People'. *American Psychology Society* 13.1 (2002): 81–84.

Dovey, Kimberly. 'Home and Homelessness: Introduction'. *Home Environments, Human Behavior and Environment: Advances in Theory and Research*, edited by Irwin Altman and Carol M. Werner, 33–64. New York: Plenum Press, 1985.

Hofstetter, Patrick, Michael Madjar and Toshisuke Ozawa. 'Happiness and Sustainable Consumption: Psychological and physical rebound effects at work in a tool for sustainable design Patrick'. *Int J LCA* 11.1 (2006): 105–115.

Ingold, Tim. *Being Alive: Essays on Movement, Knowledge and Description.* London: New York: Routledge, 2011.

Liebmann, Marian. *Art Therapy for Groups: A handbook of themes and exercises.* Hove: New York: Bruner-Routledge, 2004.

Liebmann, Marian. *Art Therapy for Groups: A handbook of themes and exercises.* Hove: New York: Bruner-Routledge, 1986.

Lusebrink, Vija B. and Palo Alto. 'Art Therapy and the Brain: An Attempt to Understand the Underlying Processes of Art Expression in Therapy'. *Art Therapy Journal of the American Art Therapy Association* 21.3 (2004): 125–135.

Malchiodi, Cathy A. *The Art Therapy Sourcebook 2nd Edition.* Hove: New York: Bruner-Routledge, 2007.

Malchiodi, Cathy A. *The Handbook of Art Therapy.* New York: The Guilford Press 2003.

Nakamura, Jeanne and Mihalyi Csikszentmihalyi. 'The Concept of Flow'. *Handbook of Positive Psychology*, edited by Charles R. Snyder and Shane J. Lopez, 89–105. Oxford: Oxford University Press, 2002.

Robson, Colin. *Real World Research: A Resource for Social Scientists and Practitioner – Researchers 3rd Edition.* Oxford: Blackwell Publishers ltd, 2011.

Rubin, Judith. *The Art of Art Therapy: What Every Art Therapist Needs to Know.* Routledge: New York: East Sussex, 2011.

Sanders, Elizabeth and Pieter Jan Stappers. 'Co-creation and the new landscapes of design'. CoDesign 4.March, (2008): 5–18.

Silverstone, Liesl. Art Therapy Exercises: Inspirational and Practical Ideas to Stimulate the Imagination. London: Jessica Kingsley Publishers, 2009.

Voytilla, Amy. 'Flow states during art making'. MA dissertation, The School of the Art Institute of Chicago, 2006

CHAPTER 7

What Is the Good Life: an Overview of the 'Good Life' at the University of Florida

Sarah A. Bushey

Abstract

Universities in the United States have increasingly integrated general humanities classes into the college curriculum. In some cases, students are required to take one if not more of these classes and the justifications include attempts to expose students to the humanities as well as to promote and demonstrate the value of an education that incorporates them. As an instructor/assistant director of a class that asks students to consider what the good life is, I would like to share my experiences over the past two years with this course and the struggle with this complex question, which includes an examination of the difference between pleasure and happiness. The class consists of various modules and there is approximately one module each week. For example, in 'Seeking the Good Life', we read Hermann Hesse's *Siddhartha* and reflect on different stages of a journey through life, different paths one may take and what they may entail, and whether or not a journey should be considered meaningful only when the destination is reached. In 'Embodying the Good Life', we read about and discuss differences of gender, belief systems, race, and also discuss issues of body image and what the social constructions of the 'ideal' body type mean to different people and how the image is marketed, displayed, and consumed. A related module is 'Owning the Good Life', where we read about Aboriginal art and issues that arise when culture becomes commodified. One of the most challenging aspects of the course is making the material relatable to the students and their lives outside the classroom, and one of the most successful ways to do that includes the incorporation of social media. The course further seeks to promote the idea that discovering what the good life is might very well happen outside the classroom rather than inside.

Keywords

happiness – higher education – humanities courses – good life

Introduction

So just what is a good life, anyway? If you had to create a list of all the things required for a person to live a good life, what would they be? This is usually the very first question I pose to my students in the course I teach, which is entitled 'What is the Good Life'. If further asked to narrow down a definition of a good life to one word, almost everyone comes up with the same one: happiness. Of course, this always leads to another question—that being, 'what is happiness?' While not everyone agrees on the same definition of happiness, some general ideas usually present themselves. In order to be happy, one must have basic necessities to live which include food, water, shelter, and, some would argue, love. Relationships are big too—everyone loves to mention family and friends and romantic relationships. Perhaps a career you love is another requirement, because after all, how can your life be happy if you hate your job? But how many of these things bring true happiness, and how many of them bring pleasure? Is happiness and pleasure the same thing?

The difference between happiness and pleasure, as Joel Kupperman argues in his book *Six Myths about the Good Life*, is one of permanence versus temporariness. Pleasures lasts a short time and also are associated with an object, while happiness is long-term and comes about for no particular reason; it is more like a state of being.[1] Can a person have one without the other? Can a person be happy without pleasure or experience pleasure without being happy? Many students, particularly in American culture, tend to believe that the best life to strive for is the one filled with the most pleasure and the least amount of pain. This kind of life would undoubtedly resemble the typical American dream: go to school, go to college and attain a higher degree, graduate, get a job, get married, and have children. In this process, earning a significant amount of money would be a goal, since pleasure is mainly brought about through objects and those objects are usually attached to a monetary value (cars, houses, boats, television, etc.). And so, we reach the point of discovering why my students are sitting in this classroom, grumbling because they are required to take this class—a class that asks them to consider some of the most fundamental and salient questions about what it means to be human and why we should care about living the happiest, healthiest, and most 'good' life possible while we are on this planet.

---

1 Joel Kupperman, *Six Myths about the Good Life: Thinking about What Has Value* (Indianapolis, Hackett Publishing Company, 2006), 1–2.

Course Topics

A brief description of the course, its objectives and its structure is in order. Broadly, the course asks students to consider themselves as individuals with particular goals and beliefs but also to consider their role as an individual within larger local and global communities. Throughout the semester, we frequently run into such questions as 'How will your attempt to live what you believe is a good life affect others and vice versa?' and 'Is it acceptable for someone to live a life that they believe is good if it negatively affects another person's quality of life?' or 'How do your choices affect the lives of others?' These are tough questions to grapple with, and students often have not thought about themselves as part of a larger community to which they have obligations. The course is interdisciplinary nd cross-cultural, and it draws on the full range of human experience throughout the world and through time in attempting to address the question of what makes a life good. Through the course, students are exposed to some of the considerable humanities resources at The University of Florida such as the Harn Museum of Art, theatrical performances on campus, and the Florida Museum of Natural History.

Since all the freshmen at the university are required to take it, there are roughly 3,000 students enrolled per semester. Because of this large volume, a typical semester will include roughly six faculty members who come from the College of Liberal Arts and Sciences, the College of Fine Arts, and the College of Design, Construction, and Planning. Each faculty member lectures around 200–300 students and teaching assistants lead discussion sections in smaller classes of 20 students per class. There are currently three formats: the live version, the completely online version of the class, and a hybrid version which has all lectures online but one live discussion section per week. This latter version is the one I have been an instructor for since fall of 2015. Each week is broken down into different modules which are based around a theme and each has its own readings and videos related to that theme. For example, in 'Seeking the Good Life', we read Hermann Hesse's *Siddhartha* and reflect on different stages of a journey through life, different paths one may take and what they may entail, and whether or not a journey should be considered meaningful only when the destination is reached. In another module titled 'Embodying the Good Life', we read about and discuss differences of gender, belief systems, race, and also discuss issues of body image and what the social constructions of the 'ideal' body type mean to different people and how such an image is marketed, displayed, and consumed. A related module is called 'Owning the Good Life', where we read about Aboriginal art as well as Native American drawings and issues that arise when culture becomes commodified or when assimilation of one culture into another occurs.

One of the most difficult yet rewarding tasks in teaching a humanities class has been showing students how the materials we read in class resonate with their lives outside the classroom. For example, during a unit titled 'Constructing the Good Life', students explore mapping as an activity unique to different cultures and discuss how various cultural maps display the values and belief systems salient to the group of people creating them. I then ask them what types of things can be considered maps of their own lives, and this usually leads to a conversation about the integration of social media such as Facebook, Instagram and Twitter into their lives as means of communication and as a tool to portray themselves to others. Sometimes the conversation goes in the direction of personal vs. private information, and often the students recognize that sharing personal information in such public forums does, to some extent, influence how they interact with others.

Student Happiness Expectations

It often seems that students are coming to college with an idea of how their life is going to play out. They arrive with a notion of what they will major in and are confident that this is the path they will follow and there will be no deviation. In my experience, the Good Life course opens them up to experiencing other possibilities for their career that they may have never considered. I have had several students over the course of the last two years tell me that they realized they were unhappy with their field of study and that the class inspired them to seek out alternative careers. This is one of the most significant and useful aspects of the course, and the materials used reinforces an encouragement of exploration, learning by trial and error, and the usefulness of making mistakes in order to grow. Finally, our discussions tend to open their eyes to the fact that they cannot rely solely on themselves in their journeys, but must also interact and work with others in a community. Interaction with others is fundamental to being human.

The difficult truth about teaching a course such as this is that to many instructors in higher education, this is the kind of class that is most needed by our students in the sense that it asks them to consider these significant questions, to think critically, and to be producers of knowledge rather than consumers of it. However, the majority of students who take the course report in evaluations that it was a waste of their time, meaningless, and it should be eliminated from the curriculum altogether. Ironically, in an attempt to help students decipher what values they revere the most, what kinds of activities make them happy, and how they would go about living the best life they possibly can, we seem to have caused them to experience a 'bad' life. Students appear to want to go through college with blinders on—just taking the classes that they need to take in order to get their degree and not stop to fully immerse themselves in an experience that, in most cases, only happens once. It has become a rarity for a student to go through college and take classes in something he or she may be interested in that is not related to their major. With this emphasis on the destination and the accompanying implication that the journey is just something to 'get through' and not something to enjoy as an experience, students are not always allowing themselves to fully explore the vast realm of options available to them.

One of the most popular videos we watch is actually a commencement speech made by David Foster Wallace called 'This Is Water'. Wallace discusses the dangerous aspect of a college education, which, he believes, enables our ability to 'over-intellectualize stuff' and to get lost in abstract arguments inside our heads instead of simply paying attention what is going on in front of us and what is happening inside of us.[2] He says:

> ... I submit that this is what the real value of your liberal-arts education is supposed to be about: How to keep from going through your comfortable, prosperous, respectable adult life dead, unconscious, a slave to your head and to your natural default-setting of being uniquely, completely, imperially alone, day in and day out.[3]

Students frequently say that this speech is one of the highlights of the class—yet when it comes to practicing or putting into effect what Wallace keeps talking about, it's another story. The idea that wealth, acquisition of material possessions, and power equal happiness is something we deal with many times throughout the semester and in various readings. One of the first that touches upon it is an excerpt from Herodotus's *The History* which centres around an interaction between Croesus, King of Lydia, and Solon, a wise man from Athens. Croesus is a very wealthy and powerful man, so naturally when he gives Solon a tour of all his riches and then asks Solon who he believes is the most blessed man, he believes Solon will name him. However, Solon names Tellus as the most blessed because he lived in a city that was well ruled, he saw his sons grow

---

2   David F. Wallace, 'This Is Water: Some Thoughts, Delivered on a Significant Occasion, about Living a Compassionate Life' (Commencement Speech at Kenyon College, Gambier, Ohio, 2005).
3   Wallace, 'This Is Water'.

up to become fine men and have families, and he died in old age while fighting bravely in defence of his city, which commemorated his bravery with a memorial in his honour. Croesus is not happy with this answer, and so he asks Solon who he would consider the second most blessed man, again expecting that Solon will name him. However, Solon responds naming the brothers Cloebis and Biton, who put on the yoke of oxen and when the oxen were not available and carried their mother into Argos for a festival to honour the goddess Hera. Thanking her sons for their act of piety, their mother asked the goddess to bless her sons with the best gift humans could receive. The goddess honoured them by killing them so that they would be spared human misery. The story of the exchange between Solon and Croesus demonstrates two significant ideas that are explored throughout the course: 1.) Wealth and power do not necessarily make one the happiest or most blessed person, and 2.) There are cultures and belief systems that advocate that a person's life cannot be considered blessed or good until after it has ended.

The tension between what we as educators believe our students need and what they themselves believe they need is ongoing. There is a lifestyle pattern that is ingrained in American students that generally consists of what can be considered 'American dream' ambitions: school, career, family and wealth somewhere in there. Perhaps these are the basic requirements in order to live a happy and 'good' life? It seems very obvious that one would pursue a career in something that inspires passion within them and makes them motivated to get out of bed day. However, the pressure and willingness to make a lot of money or be financially stable at the detriment of overall happiness should not be underestimated.

In Relation to My Own Happiness

I would like to speak briefly about my own experiences in higher education and about how teaching this course has made me profoundly question my own career choice. I was never largely concerned with making money, and my choice of a major in college as an undergraduate reflected that: I chose music education. Student teaching elementary school students was one of the most terrifying and least pleasant experiences of my life, and I knew I could never do that. Teaching high school was much better, but I still did not see myself doing it long term. I went on to graduate school for performance degree in clarinet. I completed the degree and gave a recital, but I knew I would never make a living just performing, nor did I want to; I had always been bothered by performance anxiety. I remained at the University of Florida and began pursuing a doctoral degree in musicology. This degree would take me six years to complete and would test every part of my being—physical, mental and emotional strength. Many of my close relationships were strained as well. The amount of pressure, anxiety, fear and loneliness I experienced during my doctoral years was like nothing I had ever known. I finally graduated in spring of 2015, yet had sent in close to a hundred job applications in my field and not heard back from any of them. Things looked pretty grim.

Luckily, I had been a Teaching Assistant for the Good Life course for two years, and the course director asked me to be the Assistant Director. I'd already had lots of experience with the class, and I actually enjoyed teaching it more than I enjoyed teaching music classes. It was more about looking at the big picture in life, and that was something I'd always felt was important, but it is very easy to get away from that in academia and particularly in graduate school. I took a good look at myself and realized that I had been so afraid to do anything I loved for so long and had been transformed by graduate school into a person who felt trapped in an academic box. All my ambitions of doing anything other than something inside of academia had been banished. I needed a change. I needed a change in my mental attitude and in all the bad habits I had learned as a student. I found a fitness community and began working out every day and following a healthy meal plan. I dove into all the challenge groups on social media and made connections with other like-minded people who were doing the program. I became a fitness coach to some of my immediate family members and some friends, and I found it was fun and fulfilled me in a way academic work never had. I had finally found something that gave my life real purpose and meaning, and it was located outside of academia. It was through teaching this course myself that I was able to realize that I was not being completely fulfilled in my own field of research and that something was missing.

Conclusion

Teaching the Good Life course made me realize that I have not been living a life that has been challenging enough or satisfying enough. After 12 years and 3 degrees in music, that field has not managed to hold my complete attention as a long-term career path. The reason for this is that I do not feel that I have been helping others through academic work, but I feel that I have through teaching, fitness and coaching. Grant Cardone wrote the following, and it aptly sums up how I felt about my academic career in restrospect:

> I spent 17 years getting a formal education that was to prepare me for the world—and not one course was on success. Not once did anyone talk to me about the importance of success, much less what I had to do in order to get it. Amazing! Years of education, information, hundreds of books, time in class, and money, yet I was still missing a purpose.[4]

Ultimately, my students and I usually end up agreeing that living a 'Good Life' needs to include some sense of purpose, and that cannot always be achieved if you are living your life selfishly. Motivational speaker Tony Robbins often says, 'the secret to living is giving', and that thought has recently become something I try to live my life by. The secret to living is to actually practice and enforce those things that you know will make you happier and to resist the pressure to 'buy into' what society says will make you happy, which, in American culture, almost always includes money and material possessions. In the end, happiness may look different for everyone, but there's a good chance that it will include living a life with purpose, passion and for something larger than oneself.

Bibliography

Cardone, Grant. *The 10X Rule: The Only Difference between Success and Failure*. New Jersey: John Wiley and Sons, Inc. 2011.

Kupperman, Joel. *Six Myths about the Good Life: Thinking about What Has Value*. Indianapolis: Hackett Publishing, 2006.

Wallace, David F. 'This Is Water: Some Thoughts, Delivered on a Significant Occasion, about Living a Compassionate Life'. Commencement Speech at Kenyon College. Gambier, Ohio, 2005.

---

4 Grant Cardone, *The 10X Rule: The Only Difference Between Success and Failure* (New Jersey, John Wiley and Sons, Inc., 2011).

CHAPTER 8

The Vocation Fulfilment: a Driver for Happiness at Work

Andrea-Mariana Marian and Valeriu Budeanu

Abstract

Some cultures encourage the discovery of the people's vocation since early life stages. In the case of young people – for which the job they are performing coincides with their calling – we observed a precocious maturity and another kind of foundation for their principles, main goals and set of values, including those related to work. Unfortunately, in the Romanian society encouraging the affirmation and the enhancement of native skills is a role that nor the family, nor the school is assuming it. It is surprising that in the interviews that we have analysed we have found relevant aspects related to the expression of the vocation, together with intense emotion of happiness. Therefore, we paid attention in our analysis to the way in which the subjects define their vocation through what we call interpretative repertoires, to how they build their position in relation to third parties, to how the manifestation of the inborn skills becomes extremely important within the work performed. Other relevant outcomes from the interviews are connected to the relation between vocation and motivation, vocation and financial satisfaction, about how the interviewees are reporting themselves to happiness, in general. In connection with two important issues for any company – the motivation to be employed on a certain position and the interest shown by the companies for awareness and expression, by the employees, of their own vocation – we were surprised to discover a series of staying aside attitudes related to the internal relations between the employee's vocation, happiness at the work place, involvement in achieving and exceeding the targets in the companies where those people were employed. Our research can be an important starting point for the development of the human resources management in those companies that have established as main scope: the design and the implementation of sustainable development strategies.

Keywords

vocation – happiness – interpretative repertoires – positioning – employee – company – sustainable development

1 Introduction

In our previous research,[1] we had highlighted a group of factors which have impact on the subjects' happiness. One of the happiness causes that had been identified by the persons that we have interviewed at that time was the *vocation*, seen as *the possibility to manifest, plenary, a professional calling*. We wanted to take now one more step further, in order to better understand how the mechanisms related happiness and vocation function.

2 Conceptual Framework

'Vocation' is a word from Latin (vocátio, -ónis), which has the meaning of 'calling'. Until the xvith century 'vocation' was used to designate the 'divine calling', or, with other words, the 'call' given by God to a human being which so was gifted with a talent (or several talents).

In the field of sociology the first to use the term 'vocation' was Max Weber (1864–1920), in two of his late works: 'Science as a Vocation'[2] (1918) and 'Politics as a Vocation'[3] (1919). In these two papers Weber discusses two particular cases: the benefits and detriments of choosing a career as an academic at a university who studies science or humanities and the description of the politician, respectively.

There are several theories concerned about the evaluation of the level of happiness in several contexts. We want to mention one of these theories, which best suites our research, based on the idea that happiness is attained while a person is engaged in activities and processes. This is the theory of the Hungarian origin researcher, Mihaly Csikszentmihalyi. His assumption is that people are happier when they engage in activities which awaken their interest and during which they are able to practice their skills. He named this state: flow.[4] When solving high demanding challenges by appealing to high demanding abilities, the person is in the flow.

---

1 Andrea-Mariana Marian and Valeriu Budeanu, 'The Analysis of the Causes of Employees' Happiness', (Oxford: Inter-Disciplinary Press, forthcoming).
2 Max Weber, 'Science as a Vocation', *From Max Weber: Essays in Sociology*, ed. and trans. H. H. Gerth and C. Wright Mills (New York: Oxford University Press, 1946).
3 Max Weber, 'Politics as a Vocation', *From Max Weber: Essays in Sociology*, ed. and trans. H. H. Gerth and C. Wright Mills (New York: Oxford University Press, 1946).
4 Mihaly Csikszentmihalyi, 'Flow, The Secret to Happiness', *TED*, 2004, Viewed on 18 September 2014, https://www.ted.com/talks/mihaly_csikszentmihalyi_on_flow.

3 Accomplishing the Vocation, Generating Happiness

We have conducted a qualitative research, based on: nine semi-structured interviews, recorded using a recorder and later transcribed, and eight questionnaires, with opened questions. The age range of the respondents was between 8 to 86 years, the mean age being 48 years. The professions of the respondents varied from students to economists and engineers, from priest to legal advisor and researchers.

Making enjoyable activities on a daily basis, by chance, a person can get to have a hobby. We asked ourselves 'How does this mechanism function?' And when we have analysed the interpretative repertoires[5] of the respondents to our research we were able to understand that *pleasure* leads to *desire*, which develops increased *pleasure*. The increased pleasure stirs *passion*, which in turn is leading to *hobby*. From our research resulted that in such cases, the respondents do things with *passion*, which represents the feeling one is experiencing when an activity is done with pleasure. Passion is a combination of enthusiasm and commitment, the main ingredient for all activities to come out better and even perfect. Passion determines the loss of personal self and total dedication to working;[6] and is often depicted as the living which maintains the effort required to achieve a goal.

On the other hand, the *hobby* refers to one or more activities that give the person practicing it a special pleasure and/or makes the person to relax and to rest. A hobby is performed during the spare time, occasionally, a few hours a week or on a daily basis. Our respondents also mentioned a state of peace in which the person feels a connection with God when being committed in the hobby practicing.

However, there are some causes which slow down the passion and inhibit the attainment of the hobby, like the lack of spare time, poor health, strong stress and negative emotions. In time, the passion can be lost, and also the manifestation of the hobby. What is important to note when doing things with passion is that the person forgets about the daily worries and responsibilities and he/she ignores whether there is or there isn't recognition or appreciation from the social environment.

When performing the activities related to hobby, the intensity of *pleasure* increases and leads to the awareness of a *dormant vocation*. From our survey,

---

5   Jonathan Potter and Margaret Wetherell, *Discourse and Social Psychology. Beyond Attitudes and Behaviour* (Beverly Hills: SAGE Publications, 1987), 138.
6   Csikszentmihalyi, 'Flow: The Secret to Happiness'.

results indicated that the age when one can become conscious about his/her vocation could be:
a) In the artistic field, for example, one person could realize his/her talents and value from the age of four or five, while the vocation can occur in adolescence.
b) Failing to identify one person's talents, the consciousness about vocation can occur when one decides to take responsibility for everything that happens in his/her life, which was explicitly mentioned in our research to be around the age of thirty.

The awareness of a dormant vocation increases the intensity of the passion, which is transforming the vocation into active state (choosing a profession). This is the most critical period in the intensity of the pleasure. During this period, two trends appear related the intensity of the manifestation of passion: decrease in the intensity of the passion or increase in the intensity of the passion.

The factors which were mostly mentioned in our study as being responsible for *the diminishment of the passion* and which obstruct the identification of the vocation are:
a) The family, which does not provide support;
b) A poor, primitive, isolated and dogmatic economic, social and cultural environment;
c) The desire to earn money, at any cost, which leads to the lack of interest for identification of the vocation and also influences the career choices;
d) The comfort: 'I chose to be a teacher as I do not like physical work, and is more comfortable to sit at a desk ...' (interview quote)
e) The lack of interest in doing important things for personal development, lack of long term objectives;
f) Relative pleasure and the option for easy work;
g) Youth and lack of practical experience, lack of information related vocation, and especially naivety in choosing the high education studies and in choosing a profession;
h) Life overwhelmed by solving the current needs.

The main effects on profession, when the passion is diminishing, especially when the profession was chosen due to monetary benefits, consist of:
− A monotonous activity, without enthusiasm, full of dissatisfaction, followed by demotivation at work;
− A low efficiency: the efficiency decreases from 50% -60% (about 30% of responses) to mediocre and weak (about 30% of responses); weaker (approximately 30% of responses) and even disastrous;

- Completing worthless actions and waste of all kinds of resources;
- Feel a lack of energy which makes the person tired quickly;
- Requirement of a double consumption of energy that affects the person both in the profession and during his/her leisure;
- In the human relationships lot of difficulties happen and even feelings of irritations against the others (there are people who blame anyone for their unhappiness);
- Loss of personal essence and transformation into a computer (a machine).

At the end, the personal suffering from the emotional and financial layers can turn into a riot on himself/herself as an individual and one can fall into depression or even worse, into personal failure.

The increase in the intensity of passion requires as condition for the transformation into active vocation an *educated ambition*. If a person is ambitious, it is much easier to go to performance. However, if the ambition is not educated, one cannot do anything.

We have identified a *loop of tasks* carried by a person for which a hobby transforms into *active vocation*. The steps of this loop are:

a) Implementation of experiments;
b) Engage in the task: submission of greater efforts and overcoming the difficulties aroused;
c) Increase of the person's confidence that the job suits him/her;
d) Carrying out personal research;
e) Desire for self-improvement;
f) Perseverance in applying the own methods in the activity;
g) The goal is to obtain very good results;
h) The social recognition of results and merits;
i) The decision to choose a profession and to actively practice it.

There are several signs of an *active vocation*. The person wants to do it, no matter the issues occurred. This is why she/he is willing to allocate a bigger fund of time, as the person likes to discover, to investigate and finds his/her happiness in these things. Also, the signs of the first results appear, indicating that the individual is turning to performance. This makes the person wanting to get skilled in that particular domain.

There are several types of vocation, which are unrelated with talent and which derive from hobby, like:
- Aviator – the pleasure to travel, to fly;
- Skydiving instructor – the pleasure to land by parachute;
- Diver and lifeguard – the pleasure to swim;
- Animal Trainer – the pleasure of caring for animals;
- Doctor – the pleasure of caring for people;

– Researcher – the pleasure of studying.

On the other hand, there are several vocations derived from talents, like, for example: writer, painter, voice singer, instrumental singer, dancer, wood or glass processer, sculptor, jeweller.

We were able to identify two situations when combining *a passion* with *talent*. In one case the oratorical talent with the passion for doing research in areas such as mathematics, history, geography will make a person to become a teacher. In the second case, the oratorical talent put together with the passion for research in the applied juridical sciences will lead a person to become a lawyer.

There are several criteria which differentiate the vocation from hobby, like the time frame when the vocation is discovered; the amount of time one person is allocating and the interest he/she gives to each of them; the intensity of feelings (happiness, love, spiritual energy, appreciation, esteem, gratitude) felt when the two are developed.

Increase in the intensity of passion transforms the passion into *dedication*. Dedication, as part of the vocation, has a major impact on the profession, because the profession, in general, occupies much of ones' life and a big majority of the week time. The effects of dedication on the profession, as resulted from our study are:

a) Achieve performance, excel and feel like going to reach perfection, is ideal;
b) It drives you, motivates you and makes you feel energized;
c) It gives you satisfaction and fulfilment, helping you in increasing the quality of life;
d) It helps a lot in choosing the profession and in the possibility of building a successful career;
e) It will make you happy professionally;
f) It ensures you recognition from the part of the socio-economic, cultural and professional environment, but in your turn, you produce a major positive impact on the others around you;
g) It gives you the pleasure of doing a certain thing;
h) You are 'the right man in the right place'; you become more efficient, increase your initiative and stimulate your innovative character.

The efficiency in work for a person with vocation and total dedication in the job he/she performs is excellent. The people with vocation manage to overcome hardships appeared in their profession with great power. Vocation offers to an individual:

– Balance;
– The certainty of the value of work;
– Diminishes the adverse effects that arise in situations of crisis;
– Helps the person not to suffer so much;

- Gives confidence;
- Gives energy;
- Strengthens the hope to overcome the hard times and to look forward a better period to come.

A *conflict* arises when the vocation is discovered, but the person can't practice that profession. This leads to *unhappiness*. Some examples – as they emerged from our study are:

a) 'I am not receiving confidence and freedom to do what I want!' (interview quote)
b) Envy blocks vocations very much: 'They do not realize what it means to have a man with vocation and how big added value he can bring you!' (interview quote)
c) Discontent appears at a time;
d) The person starts to crave for the vocation which he/she has, but which he/she cannot accomplish;
e) All these conflicts are beginning to translate into some frustrations.
f) In the end, it generates a state of terrible unhappiness!

Related to the intensity of the conflict, all the answers showed a very powerful conflict – because the individual is frustrated that he/she can no longer continue the work that made him happy before. An exception was one answer, which mentioned a mid-level intensity of the conflict: a person may only feel discomfort during the new activity.

When we asked the question: 'People who fulfil their vocation are happy people?' The answers we received were affirmative answers in 82% of the cases. Some example of answers from the interviews: 'He is happy because he has fulfilled his vocation'. 'This is your joy and your happiness! That you have not lived in vain on Earth, you did something important! And you can die at peace!'; 'If you work at something you think is your vocation, it makes you easier to be effective and then also to be happy!' (quotes from the interviews).

When we asked our respondents 'Which are the degrees of intensity of happiness felt by a person during the work performed if his/her vocation overlaps the profession he/she performs?' Two third of the answers noted 'strong happiness' and one third of the answers mentioned 'very strong happiness'.

The social recognition of the work's results ensures the materialization of vocation. This generates happiness and increases the energy, which in turn causes the increase of working power and maximizes efficiency. Happy people at work are powerful persons in front of any difficulties arisen in the profession, because: happiness relaxes the body and helps in making the right decisions in difficult situations; happiness determines the increase in personal confidence and happiness gives patience.

4 Conclusions

Discovering and knowing the vocation in early life stages may radically change, in good, the destiny of the person, being the best choice for the individual training of this person in their chosen field: vocation becomes the soul of the profession. The vocation is a source of happiness for each person, ensuring continuous happiness, lifting the intensity of happiness.

Happiness, in turn, increases the self-confidence and helps overcome the emotions of fear; ensures efficient and effective use of personal resources available; it is one of the ingredients of personal satisfaction and fulfilment; ensures personal success; helps in completing high quality work. Happiness also facilitates human relationships, brings more openness and tolerance, and, on the other hand, provides a person with more freedom.

Bibliography

Csikszentmihalyi, Mihaly. 'Flow: The Secret to Happiness'. *TED*, 2004. Viewed on 18 September 2014. https://www.ted.com/talks/mihaly_csikszentmihalyi_on_flow.

Potter, Jonathan and Margaret Wetherell. *Discourse and Social Psychology. Beyond Attitudes and Behaviour*. Beverly Hills: SAGE Publications, 1987.

Weber, Max. 'Politics as a Vocation'. *From Max Weber: Essays in Sociology*, Translated and edited by H. H. Gerth and C. Wright Mills, 77–128. New York: Oxford University Press, 1946.

Weber, Max. 'Science as a Vocation'. *From Max Weber: Essays in Sociology*, Translated and edited by H. H. Gerth and C. Wright Mills, 129–156. New York: Oxford University Press, 1946.

CHAPTER 9

Classic Cars and Happiness: a Profile of Participants and Their Family, Community and Cultural Health

Bryon Martin

Abstract

Research concerning happiness is well documented in the scholarly literature. Happiness is a human goal and achieving it is high on the list of human needs. However, few studies have been devoted to happiness and the involvement and participation in classic car recreation. Activities such as restoration, cruise-ins and shows, and family activities are all contexts in which the classic car enthusiasts are active. A dearth in the literature exists in regard to the systematic evaluation of how happiness is a sought and/or achieved by these participants. The current research has been undertaken to develop a social-behavioral profile of classic car enthusiasts and to ascertain the motivations and benefits of participation in the unique activity of classic car recreation in the scope of happiness. Specifically, the research aim, through a qualitative interpretive and phenomenological lens, was to identify the predominant themes that arise from structured personal interviews with and survey data collected from classic car owners. Results indicated participant involvement in classic car leisure activities contributes to happiness in numerous ways. Themes gleaned from this current research include service to community, family bonding, connection with history, identity formation, socialization, and happiness. Further examination of these themes is the aim of this research and the analysis may shed light on how and why happiness may be achieved through participation in the recreation activity of classic car collecting, restoring, and showing.

Keywords

recreation – classic car – happiness – cultural health

1   Value of Recreation

For the purposes of this research, classic car recreation includes restoring of the car, displaying the car at shows, learning information on cars, and sharing the car with others (friends, family, and community). The existing scholarly literature concerning classic car recreation is scant at best thus presenting a uniquely applicable opportunity for expansion. For this research, the overall goal was to form meanings and interpretations of the responses by the participants in relation to their happiness. The specific purpose of this chapter is to develop a social-behavioral profile of classic car enthusiasts and to ascertain the motivations and benefits of participation in the unique activity of classic car recreation in the scope of happiness.

Much research has been devoted to the study of recreation in society. However, little study has been devoted to the activity of classic car recreation and more specifically the role of the activity in the happiness of the individual. This chapter attempts to contribute to the understandings happiness through this lens.

Benefits of recreation participation include opportunities for relaxation, pleasure, cultural discovery, hobby activities, and fun. The study of recreation, in itself, is interdisciplinary and is much aligned with fields of health, sport, sociology and psychology among others.

One form of recreation involves Classic car recreation or recreation involving cars that are old (20–25 years for legal classification in most states), historical, unique, or worth restoring. In this vein, participants within a car community strive for the authentic-that is they are romanticized by the creative and cathartic opportunity to express themselves and their possession to relevant others in contrast to everyday life in a pleasurable, fun, and fantasy realm.[1]

Researchers have noted that motivations of participation in recreation are varied in scope. Humans have a desire to express creativity. Humans have a need to be social by making new friends and by engaging in group settings. A need to get away from work and explore new environments, self-discovery, and to engage in physical stimulation are also reasons people recreate. If people are able to achieve diminished stress they will be happier. The body measures happiness levels and emotional well-being and thus the absence of stress and anger, leads to positive feelings and a longer and happier life.

> In a sense, *recreation represents a fusion between play and leisure* ... the term itself stems from the Latin word *recreatio*, meaning that which refreshes or restores. Historically, recreation was often regarded as a period

---

1 Thomas W. Leigh, et al., 'The Consumer Quest for Authenticity: The Multiplicity of Meanings within the MG Subculture of Consumption,' *American Journal of Marketing Science, Vol. 34.* (2006): 481–493.

of light and restful activity, voluntarily chosen, that permits one to regain energy after heavy work and to return to work renewed.[2]

2 Participant Interviews and Survey

The focus of this research is ethnographically based. The goal of the researcher was to become immersed within the culture of classic car recreation to fully understand the underpinnings of the recreation activity. Researchers utilize the ethnographic approach in order to gain an understanding of the big picture of the inside and outside views a certain recreation activity.[3]

Characteristics of the ethnographic research employed in this study include an aim of discovery in which interviews were conducted in the initial stages of the study thus yielding conclusions from which direction for further examination through survey administration could take place. The opportunity for description of the current state of the recreation activity in terms of motivations and benefits could be achieved.

Of the participants, 68% indicated a mentor(s) had taught them the intricacies of working with and the enjoyment of classic cars. The most predominant mentor indicated by participants was father followed by friends. In regard to passing the car down, (or on to someone else after death) 79% of the participants indicated that they would and 50% indicated they would pass it on to either a son (or sons) or daughter or daughters.

For the interviews, data were collected via written field notes and voice recordings of informal conversations and unstructured interviews. Voice recorded interviews were transcribed by the researcher to determine common themes of familial, community, and cultural benefits and motivations of classic car recreation participation.

In regard to the written survey, the research goal was to build demographic descriptions of participants and ascertain the most predominant motivations for classic car recreation participation and highest ranked benefit in regard to happiness. Participants were asked to indicate all of their motivations (items derived through interview analysis) for participating in classic car recreation activities.

Participants in this study were members of a classic automobile club near a metropolitan city in the Midwest of the United States. Of the participants, valid

---

2 Daniel D. McLean, Amy R. Hurd, and Nancy Brattain Rogers, *Recreation and Leisure in Modern Society* (London: Jones and Bartlett, 2005), 38.
3 Carol Cutler Riddick and Ruth Russell, *Research Methods: How to Conduct Research in Recreation, Parks and Tourism* (Urbana, IL: Sagamore, 2015), 143.

data were collected via a written survey (*n* = 38), and through semi-structured in-person interviews, (*n* = 14). For the written survey, 9 participants female, and 29 participants are male. All but two participants ranged in age from 51–85. Interviews were conducted at a classic car show and recorded using a microphone and voice recorder. Written surveys were administered during a car club meeting.

3   Themes

Themes are presented to represent similarities across the entire sample. Of the participants with valid data, the six most predominant motivational factors were *socializing, happiness, preservation of history, growth of knowledge, re-living my youth, and relief of stress*. In terms of rankings, the top three ranked motivations were *socialization, preservation of history, and happiness.*

One recreation rooted theme emerging from interviews included that of a sense of community. Random acts of kindness within one's community notably important to classic car recreation participants. Although personal benefits of recreation are widely noted in the literature, recreation should also be understood as 'contributing to the common welfare.'[4]

> Happy people have better relationships, they are healthier and have healthier children. They have fewer conflicts and are less likely to commit crimes or pollute the environment. Happy people tend to be socially responsible-they improve the communities in which they live.[5]

Participant interview responses included community involvement as a motive of recreation participation of in classic car shows. For example, these responses included: 'I am not concerned with trophies.' 'I prefer service to organizations.' 'You really realize how lucky you are and appreciate what you have-to see those kids in those wheelchairs.' 'If it ain't for a benefit, we don't go.' 'It benefits people, my wife helps with the foundation.' 'We have a disabled son, so we try to participate in anything that benefits the community.' 'We'd rather not attend a buy a trophy show-would rather do a benefit show.'

Participants noted the value of social benefits as a motive of participation in classic car recreation. 'We meet new people all of the time, we got to be really

---

4 McLean, Hurd and Rogers, *Recreation and Leisure in Modern Society*, 168.
5 *Happy*, dir. Roco Belic, Leuven: Dalton Distribution, 2013. DVD.

close with people we meet.' 'It's a social thing, a lot of fun.' 'It's a lot of fun to see women out here at the show. 'Comradery!' 'It beats sitting around the house. Men!'

For the theme family bonding, participants offered the following motives for participation: 'My Dad was my mentor.' 'I participate with my wife.' 'I go with my spouse, and she is in favour of it.' 'Celebrate buddies anniversary.' 'My family has always had cars, part of our lives.' 'Family comes first; it's not a cheap hobby.' 'My Dad was a GM man.' 'I enjoy bringing my daughter.' 'It's a family gathering atmosphere.'

For the theme of passing it on to future generations, responses included: 'I will give mine to my son.' 'Both of my daughters will get a Buick.' 'My university professor passed this Porche down to me.' 'I will give mine to my grandson.' 'They transcend time, classics keep evolving.' 'They never go away, someone will pass it down.' 'I will be buried in mine.'

In regard to the younger generation of car enthusiasts, responses included: 'The younger generation is not interested in cars, all they want to do is play video games, at least it sure seems that way.' 'I don't think the kids really appreciate the classics, not enthusiastic about them, take away their electronics.' 'Growing up, you had to work on your own car.' 'See what I bought rather than see what I built.' 'I began washing cars in front of my house at young age and soon made good money and developed a reputation.' 'I want it now, versus a little at a time, I want it new.' 'It transcends cultures.'

In one example, the model T evoked a musical response. The flow of sheet music indicated something of the emotional quality of the automotive era. Apparently these lyrics had real meaning for those who enjoyed the speed and mobility which the new technology offered. Most of the themes were light, with some semblance of humor. One of the most memorable ones was *"The Little Ford Rambled Right Along"* created by C.R. Foster and Byron Gay:

> Now Henry Jones and a pretty little queen
> Took a ride one day in his big limousine,
> The car kicked up and the engine wouldn't crank
> There wasn't any gas in the gasoline tank.
> About that time along came Nord
> And he rattled right along in his little old Ford
> And he stole that queen as his engine sang a song
> And his little Ford rambled right along.[6]

---

6 Reynold M. Wik, *Henry Ford and Grass-Roots America* (Ann Arbor, MI: University of Michigan Press, 1972), 50.

For creativity, freedom and learning new things, participants valued classic car recreation in the following ways: 'It's nice to see everyone's creation-the character of a car can be compared to an old house.' 'It's simpler, easier to work on.' 'The women do all of the mechanical stuff themselves.' 'I like the new cars, then I can modify them.' 'They are informative, always something new, been doing this for 50 years.' *'I feel totally free when I'm in my classic, it's a surreal experience.'*

4   Alignment with Happiness

Classic Car participants enjoy their club membership, the memories and heritage the experience their cars bring, and the drivability of their cars (rather than perfection). For example, in 1908, a Ford dealer in St. Louis organized "Ford Clubs" to promote sociability and sales. In a spirit of fraternity, Ford owners banded together to attend picnics, band concerts, or to go on excursions. As many as six hundred families joined in these special events. Many of these events took on a typical folksy, rural atmosphere. Best decorated, quickest change of a tire, coffee and lemonade, noisiest Ford, came from the greatest distance, 'It seemed as though the whole countryside had taken a holiday and gone A-Fording.'[7] The analysis of the pass it on generational and family leisure effect may be useful in examining reasons for the importance of participating in classic car recreation.

> Whilst it might be mildly interesting to list the reasons for your unhappiness, and quite seductive too- there's a part of us that wants to do that, I've come to realize that the true cause of unhappiness might actually be the absence of happiness.[8]

In a 2006 survey, in only 23% of American drivers said they think of their car as 'something special—more than just a way to get around,' compared with 43% who said so in 1991. The results also indicated 69% like to drive, (as opposed to it being a chore), a 10 % decrease from 1991. Among those participants, reasons included for a positive experience included relaxation, the scenery, freedom, and the ability to get around.[9] Henry Ford noted that cars, even when

---

7   Ibid.
8   Peter Jones, *How to Do Everything and Be Happy* (London: Harper Collins, 2011).
9   D'vera Cohn, 'Data Show a Dent in Americans' Love for Cars.' *Pew Research Fact Tank Report*, 1 July 2013, viewed 18 April 2016, http://www.pewresearch.org/fact-tank/2013/07/01/data-show-a-dent-in-americans-love-for-cars/.

first invented, provided opportunity for happiness. '... .it will be so low in price that no man making a good salary will be unable to own one-and enjoy with his family the blessings of hours of pleasure in God's great open spaces.'[10] Still, interview evidence from this current study concerning younger people and their "don't care" attitude suggests that car enthusiasts value their cars and the car experience as a means of obtaining happiness, although this number may be fading.

On the other hand, study participants noted that they were likely to pass their classic car down to the next generation. Cotter notes, 'I'm just so happy he's got it, ... he's one of our gang. We were so close back then, and to this day. All of us are just as happy with Doug getting the car.'[11] Whether a grandchild, nephew, niece, or even great grandchild, the need for preservation of cultural car heritage was evident in this study and poses unique questions of car appreciation for years to come.

5 Conclusion

The current research has been undertaken to develop a social-behavioral profile of classic car enthusiasts and to ascertain the motivations for participation in the unique hobby of classic car collecting and in terms of happiness benefits derived from the leisure activity. The classic car participants include women, men, the young and old, and people from different cultures. Numerous professional backgrounds are also represented in the profile. People enjoy the entire classic care recreation experience.

Motivations for classic car participation identified in this research included *socializing, happiness, preservation of history, growth of knowledge, re-living my youth, and relief of stress*. Examples of how cultural, community and family happiness is bolstered may be applicable for recreation practitioners to model in the future as a potential models for social and community change. Classic cars and recreation activities have stood the test of time and are imperative to providing wellness.

> Recreation's most obvious value is the opportunity that it provides for fun, relaxation, and pleasure through *active participation in* sports and

---

10   Wik, *Henry Ford and Grass-Roots America*, 233.
11   Tom Cotter, *The Hemi in the Barn*, eds. Lee Klancher and Leah Noel (Minneapolis: Motorbooks MBI, 2007), 204.

games, social events, cultural pursuits, and a host of hobbies and leisure involvements … . people need meaningful ways to make contact with each other in direct, open, and friendly situations.[12]

Future analysis should take note of the role of one's profession in classic car recreation as well as military veteran status and participation according to financial stability. Additional themes may be further examined through the lens of topics such as classic tractors, boats, motorcycles, and airplanes. Lastly, further study is warranted concerning the aesthetic beauty of classic cars and its effect on people in dimensions such as self-efficacy and self-actualization.

Bibliography

Cohn, D'vera. 'Data Show a Dent in Americans' Love for Cars.' *Pew Research Fact Tank Report*, 1 July 2013, viewed 18 April 2016, http://www.pewresearch.org/fact-tank/2013/07/01/data-show-a-dent-in-americans-love-for-cars/.

Cotter, Tom. Forward by Jay Leno. *The Hemi in the Barn: More Great Stories of Automotive Archaeology*, edited by Lee Klancher and Leah Noel. Minneapolis: Motorbooks MBI Publishing, 2007.

Happy. Directed by Roco Belic. Leuven, Belgium. Dalton Distribution, 2013. DVD.

Jones, Peter. *How to Do Everything and Be Happy*. London: Harper Collins, 2011.

Leigh, Thomas, Cara Peters and Jeremy Shelton. 'The Consumer Quest for Authenticity: The Multiplicity of Meanings within the MG Subculture of Consumption.' *American Journal of Marketing Science* 34 (2006): 481–493.

McLean, Daniel, Amy Hurd and Nancy Brattain Rogers. *Recreation and Leisure in Modern Society*, 7th ed. Mississauga, ON: Jones and Bartlett, 2005.

Riddick, Carol Cutler and Ruth Russell. *Research Methods: How to Conduct Research in Recreation, Parks and Tourism*. Urbana, IL: Sagamore, 2015.

Rubin, Gretchen. *The Happiness Project*. New York, NY: Harper Collins Publishers, 2009.

Wik, Reynold M. *Henry Ford and Grass-Roots America*. Ann Arbor, MI: University of Michigan Press, 1972

---

12 McLean, Hurd and Rogers, *Recreation and Leisure in Modern Society*, 168.

CHAPTER 10

Happiness and the Structure and Dynamics of Human Life

Søren Harnow Klausen

Abstract

Extant accounts of happiness and wellbeing have been insufficiently attentive to the fact that human lives have important structural and dynamic features. All the dominant theories, be it hedonism, preference or life satisfaction accounts or even Aristotelian theories of flourishing and the good life, are essentially *list* theories. They enumerate various features that might contribute to happiness, like pleasant experiences, satisfied preferences, positive judgments, personal character traits or social relations. Yet human lives are arguably more than neutral containers or bearers of things that are good and bad. The ways lives are lived and play out, the different forms they take, and the interrelations between different experiences and goods, might matter even more for happiness than the quality of the experiences, traits or events taken in isolation. I consider the view that the 'narrative' relations between events in a person's life, as well as its form, are important elements in happiness or wellbeing, and argue, more generally, for a holistic approach to both the conceptualization and the assessment of human happiness.

Keywords

nature and definition of happiness – temporal aspects of happiness – happiness and the structure of human life – happiness and narrativity – list theories of wellbeing – happiness and life trajectories

1   The Ubiquity and Shortcomings of the Enumerative Approach

The relationship between happiness, wellbeing and the good life is controversial. I will follow Haybron[1] in distinguishing between *happiness*, understood

---

1 Daniel Haybron, *The Pursuit of Unhappiness: The Elusive Psychology of Well-Being* (Oxford: Oxford University Press, 2008).

as a purely psychological notion, *wellbeing*, the normative notion of what is non-instrumentally good for a person,[2] and the *good life*, which might include further normative factors like moral goodness. However, since it is widely assumed that happiness is a central component in wellbeing, I shall treat theories of wellbeing and happiness relatively indiscriminately.

It is common to follow Parfit in distinguishing between *hedonism, preference* theories and *objective list* theories of wellbeing.[3] Yet in a way, all these theories are 'list-theories', as they conceive of wellbeing as an aggregate of discrete items, be it pleasurable experiences, instances of desire satisfaction or the realization of objective goods like achievement or friendship. Even theories that appear to sensitive to human lives as such (e.g. Aristotelian accounts) do not acknowledge the full significance of how lives are formed and unfold, or of the interaction among experiences and goods. This also holds for the influential capabilities approach.[4]

The shortcomings of the traditional enumerative approach have not gone completely unnoticed. The clearest diagnosis has been given by Velleman, who argues that wellbeing is not additive but depends on the 'narrative' relations between events.[5] Similar suggestions have been made at the periphery of what otherwise appears to be traditional enumerative approaches.[6] Hurka considers the potential value of a life's being 'well-rounded', but treats the notion with considerable reservation. Even Kahneman, whose notion of 'objective happiness' is deliberately conceived as atomistic and focuses exclusively on the experience of the present, does acknowledge that order effects are ubiquitous.[7] Hence it can be said that the holistic nature of wellbeing has been recognized, but the idea has not been worked out or brought to bear on well-being research in general.

---

2 Roger Crisp, 'Well-Being'. *Stanford Encyclopedia of Philosophy*, ed. Edward N. Zalta (Stanford: The Metaphysics Research Lab, Stanford University Press, 2015), np, viewed 20 April 2016, http://plato.stanford.edu/archives/sum2015/entries/well-being/.
3 Derek Parfit, *Reasons and Persons* (Oxford: Oxford University Press, 1984).
4 Amarty Sen, 'Capability and Well-Being', *The Quality of Life*, edited by Amartya Sen and Martha Nussbaum (Oxford: Oxford University Press, 1933), 30–66; Martha Nussbaum, *Creating Capabilities* (Cambridge, MA: Harvard University Press, 2011).
5 David J. Velleman, 'Well-Being and Time', *Pacific Philosophical Quarterly* 72 (1991): 48–77.
6 Michael Slote, *Goods and Virtues* (Oxford: Clarendon Press, 1983); James Griffin, *Well-Being* (Oxford: Clarendon, 1986), 34f.; Haybron, *The Pursuit*, 83, 99; Thomas Hurka, *Perfectionism* (Oxford: Oxford University Press, 1993); Thomas Hurka, *The Best Things in Life: A Guide to What Really Matters* (Oxford: Oxford University Press, 2011).
7 Daniel Kahneman, 'Experienced Utility and Happiness: A Moment-Based Approach'. *Choices, Values and Frames,* eds. Daniel Kahneman and Amos Tversky (New York: Cambridge University Press, 2000).

2 Forms of Wellbeing Holism

Experiential holism is the view that the phenomenal character of an experience is influenced by the phenomenal character of the other experiences with which it is co-conscious or by its relationship to those other experiences.[8] The most obvious examples are of joint *synchronic* experiences. There is something it is like to enjoy read wine; and there is something it is like to enjoy the opening of Brahm's 4th symphony. There is also something it is like to enjoy read wine *while* enjoying the opening of Brahm's 4th symphony, and this is not just a sum or aggregate of the content of the two experiences. More specifically, the 'hedonic value' of the composite experience is not simply the sum of the hedonic value of each experience taken in isolation. Maybe the wine tastes even better when accompanied by a pleasant musical experience. Less obvious, but still quite plausible, is the existence of *diachronic* holistic effects on experiences. It may be better to enjoy something sweet after enjoying something salty, rather than the other way round; or better to enjoy a sense of fulfilment after having enjoyed a sense of longing. Such relationships may be contingent, depending on culturally induced habits, or more deeply rooted in the phenomenal character of the experiences themselves. But for a given individual under given circumstances, the total hedonic value of two subsequent experiences can depend, inter alia, on the order in which they occur.

It may be thought that this kind of intra-experiential and relatively local holism can be easily accommodated by the traditional theories like hedonism. The hedonist can simply insist that happiness requires a favourable balance of pleasure over unpleasure, and remain indifferent to how much should be taken into account in order to determine the general level of pleasure of a person. Still, recognizing holistic effects makes it impossible to calculate the happiness of an individual from a simple enumeration of her component experiences. Especially diachronic holism does put views like Kahneman's moment-based approach under pressure, since it casts doubts on whether the value of temporally extended experiences can be decomposed into the value of momentary experiences.

Experiential holism does not by itself constitute any radical break with the traditional approaches to happiness and wellbeing. But it prompts us to consider more wide-ranging holistic effects. The place of an experience, event, state or character trait in a larger pattern could also matter for wellbeing. Many

---

8 Barry Dainton, *The Phenomenal Self* (Oxford: Oxford University Press 2008), 273, 277ff.

grades of such holism are possible, depending on the kind and scope of the contextual factors involved. Most extreme is the view that the overall shape of life matters for wellbeing. Maybe the end of life, or its general trajectory, the distribution of ups and downs, ambitions and achievements, can make a difference, so that two lives that contain the same number or amount of positive and negative elements could still differ with respect to their overall level of happiness. But before considering such a global life-structure holism, it will be wise to examine more restricted claims.

A fairly moderate example is this. In athletics, the third lap of a 1500 meter or mile race is widely feared as being especially challenging and painful. The actual pain may be mitigated by release of adrenalin and end endorphins, motivation and the like. Yet middle-distance runners can certify that running the third lap hurts, plainly and simply, in a way that, taken in isolation – e.g. if one focuses solely on the character of the experience – differs little from the effects of sickness or violence. Still, we do not feel sorry for a middle distance runner on the third lap in the same way we feel sorry for victims of sickness or violence. Wellbeing is arguably what we care for when we care for other people.[9] But I care less for what my son endures on the third lap of a race than I would if he were to experience similar pains by being dragged after a car as a prisoner of war.

There are, of course, significant differences between the two situations, e.g. that the pain during the race can be said to be instrumental to achieving a desired goal, whereas the pain of the prisoner will be accompanied by an experience of humiliation, fear and uncertainty. But even if we abstract from these differences and focus on the wellbeing value of the pain *as such*, it remains different in the two cases. We don't take it to be as *harmful* to the runner, even though it is equally *hurtful*. So we seem to have a clear counterexample to the view that happiness or wellbeing can be reduced to the presence or absence of positive or negative experiences.

Though this example only suffices to establish a relatively local and still moderate degree of holism, its point may be generalized in a way that leads toward a more global approach. It shows that the wellbeing value of an experience can be influenced by an activity of which it is a part. It can be more or less meaningful, acceptable or satisfying, or more or less harmful, depending on its place in a scheme of events. But then it seems plausible that activities or events can themselves be more or less meaningful or satisfying, depending on their place in a still larger scheme of events. By following this train of thought,

---

9   Stephen Darwall, *Welfare and Rational Care* (Princeton: Princeton University Press, 2002).

we are led towards a view known from existential philosophy: It it is possible to give meaning to one's life in general by choosing or acting in certain ways. If a criminal manages to change her life and goes on using her past experience as basis for positive self-development and social engagement, this might put her miserable childhood in a more positive light, as it now becomes part of a meaningful story with a relatively happy end.

3   Dynamic Aspects and Life Trajectories

It can further be argued that what matters is not just *what* happens in one's life, but also *how* one's life is lived or plays out. Lives are not mere containers or passive receptors of experiences or events. Of course, the value of activities, autonomy, freedom etc. has been acknowledged, to various degrees, by the traditional theories, by simply having items like 'engaging in meaningful activities' or 'doing something with one's life' on the list of goods.

Several ways can be envisaged in which the dynamic aspect of happiness could be conceptualized and incorporated into a comprehensive theory, in more or less radical or ambitious ways. Again, we might start with intra-experiential features. There is a special felt quality to acting, trying, struggling, succeeding, failing and the like. This has been described in recent work on the phenomenology of agency.[10] Some have suggested that there is a distinctive phenomenology of cognitive activity.[11] This may play a part in elucidating various forms of 'intellectual pleasure' that should be taken into account besides the putative effects on wellbeing that have to do with the static *possession* of knowledge.[12]

A further step is to turn to actions and events as such, i.e. go beyond the realm of experiences. We might try to combine the global, holistic approach and the dynamic perspective by focusing on *life trajectories*. This notion is borrowed from social psychology, where it typically means something like a 'sequence of socially defined events and roles that the individual enacts over

---

10   Terry Horgan, John L. Tienson and George Graham. 'The Phenomenology of First-Person Agency', *Physicalism and Mental Causation*, eds. Sven Walter and Heinz-Dieter Heckmann (Exeter: Imprint Academic, 2003); Tim Bayne, 'The Phenomenology of Agency', *Philosophy Compass* 3.1 (2008): 182–202.

11   Søren Harnow Klausen, 'The Phenomenology of Propositional Attitudes,' *Journal of Phenomenology And the Cognitive Sciences* 7 (2008): 445–462.

12   Hurka, *Perfectionism* and *Best Things in Life*.

time'.[13] Such a sequence is, however, at most contingently related to happiness and wellbeing, and the notion of a sequence of roles is obviously too coarse to capture the subtler kind of dynamics with which we are concerned. Hence the notion needs reinterpretation.

A mere temporal pattern of distribution of goods or experiences is also not what we are after. Such a pattern may be interesting to think about, and maybe in some way relevant to wellbeing. Maybe upward trends, or just stable trends, or some degree of variation, are conducive to wellbeing, which in that case would, again, be more than just the sum of momentary goods or experiences. But a pattern of distribution does not capture anything like the dynamics of *life*, which arguably include something like activity, direction, emergence or disappearance of relations of significance or relevance etc.

I have already noted that narrative relations between events might matter for wellbeing. The athletics example showed that experiences may take on different happiness or wellbeing values in the context of an activity. This indicates the importance of the overall form or structure of a life, considered as a system (and not just a pattern) of events and activities. Hurka has speculated that a life's *narrative arc* may be a relevant factor. But apart from doubts about the general significance of shapes of a purely geometrical sort (e.g. the value of 'well-roundedness' etc.), which Hurka voices himself,[14] it seems that the notion of a narrative arc is too abstract to capture the kind of subtle dynamics we are after. Happiness and wellbeing may be essentially connected to a life trajectory; but this is not just a kind of general dramaturgical structure. You can arguably live a life with rising action, climax, falling action and resolution all in place, and so meet all the dramaturgical criteria without being particularly happy. The life of tragic heroes can have the most beautiful narrative form, but this hardly makes them enviable. Hence the relevant notion of a life trajectory must be less about the outward shape of life, less about milestones and achievements as such, and more sensitive to the quality and process of living. The guiding idea is that life is lived – or moves, or unfolds – as a continuous interplay between choices, commitments, experiences and events, and that this can be seen as a certain direction or path, a certain way in which one's life is, almost literally 'going', or a way in which one is 'doing'.

---

13   Janet Z. Giele and Glen H. Elder, eds., *Methods of Life Course Research: Qualitative and Quantitative Approaches* (Thousand Oaks, CA: Sage, 1998).

14   Hurka, *Best Things in Life*, 177.

4 Challenges and Limitations

I take it to be fairly well established that some kind of holistic and dynamic approach to wellbeing is needed. But it is open to question what kind of holism is appropriate, and I am aware of a range of problems and limitations of the views I have been considering.

First, it is not unlikely that many of the effects and phenomena I have highlighted can in fact be accommodated by more or less traditional approaches, either by simply setting aside as an empirical question to what extent individual experiences or events are affected by other experiences or events, or by recognizing further types of experiences and goods.

Secondly, it is possible to argue that the holistic effects do pertain to wellbeing, but that they are irrelevant to happiness in the psychological sense. Some might argue that two persons who suffer from an equally severe pain (etc.) are in fact equally happy, but that the one of them whose experience is embedded in a positively meaningful event structure has a higher degree of wellbeing.

Thirdly, by pressing the case for holism, we are driven towards some very complicated views, which, apart from being difficult to apply to empirical research, may seem puzzling in other respects. For example, I am strongly inclined to think that happiness is objective in the sense that it is not dependent on the attitudes and judgments of the person in question; on this question, I side with hedonists and Aristotelians against proponents of preference or life satisfaction accounts. Such an objectivism is well supported by the instability and apparent unreliability of life satisfaction reports, the influence of different cultural norms of reports and self-assessments,[15] and the fact that people can obviously have the wrong desires. Yet by invoking the notion of a life trajectory, especially in the comprehensive sense in which I have proposed that we use it, we seem forced to take into account a person's commitments and preferences and consider how they match the the person's actual experiences an accomplishments.

The very notion of meaningful activity probably cannot be adequately defined without reference to the goals and values of the person who is carrying out the activity in question. We may be able to stretch *these* notions so a to make them less subjective. It might be argued that it is not so bad for a young person to suffer some inconvenience, or even pain, as long as it happens for some good reason, even if the she is unable to see the point in it herself. But unless we are prepared to make some rather heavy metaphysical assumptions,

---

15 Haybron, *The Pursuit.*

taking there to be goals and values in themselves, or flowing directly from the nature of human beings, we will probably still have to refer to someone to whom this seems, or could seem, reasonable or meaningful. Hence the move towards wellbeing holism may change our conception from being simple and objective to being not only very complicated, but also strongly normative and so perhaps relative to a specific set of interests or preferences, be it the individual's own or those of her community.

Fourthly, although the idea of 'narrative relations' may seem very intuitive, it turns out to be surprisingly difficult to cash it out. In spite of the enormous popularity of 'narrative' approaches, few definitions seem even remotely satisfying. Often narrativity is taken to mean simply conformity with some kind of narrative scheme. But as already noted, such a 'plot structure'-notion is too rigid and abstract to capture the flexible and fine-grained relations between events that are relevant for wellbeing.

Fifthly, by widening the perspective in the way suggested, we change the focus from peoples' actual, concrete, here-and-now happiness and wellbeing to more lofty ideals of what would arguably be good for them. Saying of a person who actually feels miserably right now that she is really doing good, or even happy, because she is well on the way to accomplish something valuably, can sound suspiciously like a kind of totalitarian rhetoric ('Your real happiness lies in sacrificing yourself for the people'). There is a risk of making people into slaves of the good life, if the latter is too remote from their actual nature and interests, or if realizing it will cost too much in terms of subjective discomfort. This is (the?) problem that confronts all objectivist theories of wellbeing.

Several lines of reply are possible, however. The distinction between happiness and wellbeing can be invoked, as it can be said that the holistic approach aims at constructing a notion of wellbeing beyond happiness (and so it can be admitted that the miserable person is genuinely unhappy, or at least not exactly happy). One could also follow Velleman in distinguishing two kinds of self, one synchronic and the other diachronic, and allow them to differ with respect to wellbeing (my synchronic self may suffer, and be less well off, but my diachronic self does well, since it is about to accomplish some valuable task).[16] The latter – and perhaps even the former – strategy does, however, seem to me to represent an unattractive dualism. We can, of course, do better and worse in different respects, or according to different criteria. But we should be able to give a single, unambiguous answer to the question of how an individual is doing at a given time.

---

16   Velleman, 'Well-Being and Time'.

Hence I think that a better response is simply to acknowledge the risk and decide to take appropriate care. We should not measure the lives of individuals against standards that are alien to what can reasonably be taken as their own interests and own good. This does not compel us to roll back the movement towards holism and retort to something like moment-based hedonism or preference-satisfaction theory. We should indeed focus on the ways lives are lived and played out; but in doing so we must, of course, also take care that these are really significant features of the actual lives of the actual persons with which we are concerned.

Bibliography

Bayne, Tim. 'The Phenomenology of Agency'. *Philosophy Compass* 3.1 (2008): 182–202.

Crisp, Roger. 'Well-Being'. *Stanford Encyclopedia of Philosophy*. 2015, np. Viewed 20 April 2016. http://plato.stanford.edu/archives/sum2015/entries/well-being/.

Dainton, Barry. *The Phenomenal Self*. Oxford: Oxford University Press, 2008.

Darwall, Stephen. *Welfare and Rational Care*. Princeton: Princeton University Press 2002.

Giele, Janet Z. and Glen H. Elder, eds. *Methods of Life Course Research. Qualitative and Quantitative Approaches*. Thousand Oaks, CA: Sage, 1998.

Griffin, James. *Well-Being*. Oxford: Clarendon, 1986.

Haybron, Daniel M. *The Pursuit of Unhappiness: The Elusive Psychology of Well-Being*. Oxford: Oxford University Press, 2008.

Horgan, Terry, John Tienson and George Graham. 'The Phenomenology of First-Person Agency'. *Physicalism and Mental Causation*, edited by Sven Walter and Heinz-Dieter Heckmann, 323–40. Exeter: Imprint Academic, 2003.

Hurka, Thomas. *Perfectionism*. Oxford: Oxford University Press, 1993.

Hurka, Thomas. *The Best Things in Life: A Guide to What Really Matters*. Oxford: Oxford University Press, 2001.

Kahneman, Daniel. 'Experienced Utility and Happiness: A Moment-Based Approach'. *Choices, Values and Frames*, edited by Daniel Kahneman and Amos Tversky, 673–692. New York: Cambridge University Press.

Klausen, Søren Harnow. 'The Phenomenology of Propositional Attitudes'. *Journal of Phenomenology And the Cognitive Sciences* 7 (2008): 445–462.

Nussbaum, Martha C. *Creating Capabilities*. Cambridge, MA: Harvard University Press, 2011.

Parfit, Derek. *Reasons and Persons*. Oxford: Oxford University Press, 1984.

Sen, Amartya. 'Capability and Well-Being'. *The Quality of Life*, edited by Amartya Sen and Martha C. Nussbaum, 30–66. Oxford: Oxford University Press, 1993.

Siegel, Susanna. 'Cognitive Penetrability and Perceptual Justification'. *Noûs* 46 (2012): 201–222.
Slote, Michael. *Goods and Virtues.* Oxford: Clarendon Press, 1983.
Velleman, David J. 'Well-Being and Time'. *Pacific Philosophical Quarterly* 72 (1991): 48–77.

CHAPTER 11

Quo Vadis: Fullness or Emptiness in the Pursuit of Happiness?

Robert D. Hermanson

Abstract

Quo Vadis? Whither goest thou? In pursuit of pleasures, places, possessions or. ... perhaps happiness? Aristotle once observed that it was a quest for fullness by observing *sublime beatitudo*: 'this category ... encompasses a reach for fullness and perfection of happiness. The fullness, therefore, of goodness, beauty, truth and love.'[1] This Western notion of happiness as a condition of fullness has permeated cultures for centuries, including those of the American scene. Jefferson's usage of the terms 'life, liberty and the pursuit of happiness' tracing back to John Locke's commentaries, extends Aristotle's own observations. Consequently, and in a capitalistic society, it is also about the acquisition of things. In contrast, the notion of emptiness, an Eastern concept, provides a dialectic construct. Zhuangzi's notions of joy and particularly in the *Dao*, form a construct that engages in what he calls the 'fasting' or 'forgetting' ... an emptying out of hearts and minds of so-called 'toxic' elements of those ideals and goals that might be contaminated by the materialisms of the world. Hence, such pursuits of happiness (and joy) require the absence of things, not their acquisitions. Philosophically, and culturally, the distance between fullness and emptiness may seem very large. Perhaps it's all about who we are in terms of our own fullness, emptiness, or both, as human beings in the pursuit of happiness. However, I would argue that these often ironic conditions also have mutually shared attributes. In this chapter I should like to address both conditions, their attributes, and how they may redefine the notion of happiness within the present *zeitgeist*.

Keywords

fullness – emptiness – *sublime beatitudo* – happiness – Dao

---

1 Robert Spitzer, S.J., 'The Four Levels of Happiness,' (Bellevue WA: Catholic Education Research Center, 1999), viewed 25 January 2016, http://www.catholiceducation.org/en/religion-and philosophy/apologetics/the-four-Levels-of-happiness.html.

1 What Is Happiness?

'Happiness is a warm puppy.'[2] Charles Schulz was reflecting on that loveable beagle 'Snoopy' we all know from 'Peanuts,' his famous comic strip. An immediate pleasure to millions who have read him in the past, the notion of a simple beagle bringing smiles to an increasingly dark world, provided all of us with those fleeting moments we call happiness.

On the other hand, there are others who have observed perhaps more profound observations about happiness. Seneca once observed that 'True happiness is ... to enjoy the present, without anxious dependence upon the future.'[3] Furthermore, Osho once observed that

> Sadness gives depth. Happiness gives height. Sadness gives roots. Happiness gives branches. Happiness is like a tree going into the sky, and sadness is like the roots going down into the womb of the earth. Both are needed, and the higher a tree goes, the deeper it goes, simultaneously. The bigger the tree, the bigger will be its roots. In fact, it is always in proportion. That's its balance.[4]

Therefore, what is happiness? Is it the immediacy of a warm puppy ... a very present experience that Seneca would have endorsed? Or, is it far more complex, that which is about dualities – in Osho's terms, between sadness and happiness, depth vs. height? I would like to begin with a discussion addressing two constructs: 'fullness' and 'emptiness.' They likewise, suggest dualities, one representing Western perspectives, the other, Eastern. While seemingly in opposition, I would argue that their conditions of completeness (and existence) regarding 'happiness' mutually co-exist.

2 Fullness: Two Interpretations

Thomas Jefferson, author (with others) of the Declaration of Independence, noted for all to observe, that the document represented the rights of every

---

2 Charles M. Schulz, *Happiness is a Warm Puppy*, (Kennebunkport, Maine: Cider Mill Press, 2015), cover.
3 Lucius Annaeus Seneca, The Stoic Philosophy of Seneca: Essays and Letters, transl. Moses Hadas, (W.W. Norton & Co. New York, 1958)
4 Osho, *Everyday Osho: 365 Daily Meditations for the Here and Now*, (Gloucester, MA: Fair Winds Press, 2002).

American to enjoy the privileges to 'Life, Liberty and the pursuit of Happiness.'[5] An astounding document, now enshrined in the Archives in Washington D.C., it nevertheless has its sources in the writings of John Locke, and his colleagues[6] in England ... an enemy of the United States during the Revolutionary War of Independence.

For Jefferson, this was, nevertheless, Enlightenment material ... a break from the tyranny of the past monarchies, and a movement toward an egalitarian form of government. For Locke it was what he called 'the highest perfection of intellectual nature in a careful and constant *pursuit of true and solid happiness.*' Thus in light of the fascination with Classical Greece and Rome during this period, he returned to the notion of 'happiness' as interpreted by the Greeks as *eudaimonia* ... which is linked to *aretê*, the Greek word for 'virtue' or 'excellence.'[7]

Eudaimonia

But what is *eudaimonia* or even *aretê* really all about? In the *Ethics* Aristotle states that the term carries connotations of success and fulfillment. Thus happiness is our highest goal. In order to achieve such requires the presence of what he refers to as "virtues." So what are virtues all about? Again, for Aristotle virtue exists as a mean state between the vicious extremes of excess and deficiency (courage, for example, as between the vices of rashness and cowardice). Therefore, to be virtuous is to achieve those conditions that ultimately lead to what might be called a good character. While these are actions demonstrating virtue, what of the higher powers regarding the intellect?

For Aristotle therefore, the highest virtue is found in contemplation ... and hence the highest form of happiness, unlike our practical activities. This requires engaging teleological views of nature in which the *telos*, the goal of human life, results in the exercise of our rational powers. Of these, wisdom is the highest since it deals with unchanging universal truths, resting on a synthesis of scientific investigation. Consequently, the activity of wisdom ultimately leads to contemplation and it is here that we may fulfil both the physical as well as intellectual aspirations that ultimately lead to *eudaimonia* ... pure happiness.

---

5 Life, Liberty and the pursuit of Happiness, viewed 16 December 2015, https://wikipedia.org/wiki/Life,_Liberty_and_the_Pursuit_of_Happiness.
6 Other sources contest Jefferson's references to Locke's *Two Treatises of Government* stating that they emerged from his other document *Concerning Human Understanding*.
7 Eudaimonia (Greek: εὐδαιμονία [eu̯dai̯moníaː]), sometimes anglicized as eudaemonia or eudemonia /juːdɪˈmoʊniə/, is a Greek word commonly translated as happiness or welfare, viewed 20 December, 2015 https://en.wikipedia.org/wiki/Eudaimonia.

So where does fullness fit into this entire scenario? If we succeed in fulfilling ourselves mentally, and spiritually through the notion of *eudaimonia* we also must exist as physical beings. Aristotle points this out in several of his writings. For example he states that 'nevertheless happiness plainly requires external goods too, as we said: for it is impossible, or at least not easy, to act nobly without some furniture of fortune.'[8]

Such acquisitions assist the life of the citizen allowing him to be a significant contributor to the life of the city. Therefore, as such, the manifestations of the civic realm were reinforced and made manifest through the construction of great monuments (presumably with the taxable support of its citizens). The Parthenon, constructed during the Age of Pericles in ancient Greece for example, represents perhaps the ultimate expression of beauty manifested through architecture. Walking through this magnificent site as I did years ago (it's off limits now), I was in awe of the beauty of the place, particularly at night. We were there during the full moon when all the artificial lights were off, and only the moonlight illuminated the ruins. The place emerged as a moment that became sublime, only to be reinforced by the immediacy of the moment. It was magical! Hence, in response to Seneca's notion of the moment, it was also about happiness.

Secularization vs. Sacrilization

But what about the immediacy of the moment (and happiness) from the perspective of the Urbis ... the contemporary city? In a chapter that I presented a few years ago, I made a distinction between what I called the 'secularization vs. the sacrilization' of the urbis ... the city.[9] The two conditions would appear, within the present *zeitgeist* to be interchangeable. That is, what is considered sacred might also be considered secular and *vice versa*. The Woolworth Tower in Manhattan is a perfect example ... a skyscraper (once the highest in the world) devoted to commerce, but with the accoutrements of sacredness (an architectural gothic revival expression) and referred to by the press as a 'Cathedral of Commerce.' As J. Huizinga observed:

> It would be a mistake to think that America is materialistic because of its strong proliferation of big business, which is so manifestly embodied

---

8 Aristotle *The Nichomachean Ethics*, Fifth Edition, trans. P.H.Peters, M.A., (London: Kegan Paul, Trench, Trubner & Co., Ltd. London, 1893): 1.8,15.

9 Robert Hermanson, 'Secularization vs. Sacralization: The Paradoxical City'(paper presented at the Seventh Savannah Symposium: 'Spirituality of Place,' Savannah, GA, February 17–19, 2011).

in its skyscrapers. The substance of this reality is materialistic, no doubt, but so vehemently, so insistently, so fervently materialistic, that the very ardor of the devotion vouchsaved to the material rises to a new kind of spirituality. The impulse, overreaching itself, becomes transcendent.[10]

For Van Leeuwen then, 'the worldly powers have conquered the city, and they rule it in the robes of the Church.'[11]

But do all of these accoutrements of wealth, power and success suggest happiness? I have to return to Aristotle who defined happiness as a series of stages: *Laetus*, sensual gratification; *Felix*, ego gratification; *Beatitudo*, happiness in serving others and finally, *Sublime Beatitudo*, ultimate, perfect happiness. This final stage, the highest, achieves 'fullness, therefore, of goodness, beauty, truth and love.'[12] I should also add, through the attributes of wisdom and contemplation as well!

Is it possible to reach such a fullness or even a perfection within the present *zeitgeist*? Perhaps we need to look to another cultural framework, another construct that I call 'emptiness' for possible alternative answers.

3   Emptiness: Two Interpretations

A Shinto shrine, (jinja), is a central space hosting people's religious activities. It is also called shiro, or yashiro; and its basic principle is 'to embrace emptiness.' In its original form, four pillars were raised on the ground and their tops tied with sacred ropes, leaving an 'empty space' in the centre. Precisely because this space is designed to be 'empty,' there is always the possibility that something may enter it.[13]

The notion of 'emptiness' has several meanings. It may convey simply that which is about an empty space ... a nothingness place. In contrast, it might be all about that which is between 'things' ... therefore having its own place in the realm of things. In the Shinto shrine, it is all about potentialities ... 'that something may enter it.' But it also may connote other attributes as well.

---

10 Thomas A.P. Van Leeuwen, *The Skyward Trend of Thought*, (Cambridge, MA: MIT Press, 1988): 28
11 Van Leeuwen, *The Skyward*: 60.
12 Spitzer, 'The Four Levels of Happiness'
13 Kenya Hara, *White*, trans. Jooyeon Rhee, (Zurich: Lars Müller, 2009), viewed 25 January 2016, http://www.amazon.com/White-Kenya-Hara/dp3037781831\

Ma

This concept of that which is between 'things' may be best observed through the notion of *Ma*.[14] In Japanese culture the meaning of *Ma* pertains to the interval between two things. Interestingly, it may convey either temporal or spatial intervals, or possibly both, depending on its context.

We can observe this architecturally in the gardens of Kyoto, particularly those that reside at Ryoan-ji. Following the traditions of the Myōshin-ji school of the Rinzai branch of Zen Buddhism it represents the essence of the garden as a place of contemplation. ... a removal of the contemplator into another realm, hence between two realms ... that of the garden and that of the self in contemplation. No longer wandering in the gardens of a European style enterprise, the participant enters into a contemplative environment and is removed, mentally and spiritually. In such a realm, he or she can only contemplate the meaning of the 15 rocks, one of which is always concealed; the pebbles of sand raked daily forming a pattern around the rocks. But is this a metaphor for the sea, the rocks as mountain islands ... or something else? That is perhaps the garden's greatest contribution ... it's meaning remains an enigma.[15]

So where is the happiness in such an enigma? Perhaps we need to return to what Kawai Hayao calls the 'hollow center.' In the Japanese culture there resides the notion of the 'hollow center' which is all about emptiness. When forces confront each other on either side of this empty center, the emptiness acts as a kind of buffer zone that prevents the confrontation from growing too intense. It can thus be construed as a place not of absences, but rather presences ... filled with power and tension.[16] But it is also about resolutions that prevent confrontations. Hayao makes note of this through the juxtaposition between good and evil, and the significance of the hollow centre in establishing a kind of equilibrium.[17]

Ma then, is that emptiness that is really a fullness through equilibrium that suggests the potentiality for happiness, but not necessarily its achievement.

---

14 Gunter Nitschke, 'Ma: Place, Space, Void,' *Kyoto Journal* 8, (1988) viewed 10 January 2016, http://www.kyotojournal.org/the-journal/culture-arts/ma-place-void/

15 Marc Treib, and Mark Herman, 'Ryoan-ji,' *A Guide to the Gardens of Kyoto*, (New York: Kodansha America, Inc., 2003): 93–95.

16 Isao Kumakura, 'The Culture of Ma,' *Japan Echo*, 34:1, 2007, viewed 31 July 2015, http://www.japanecho.com/sum/2007/340114.html

17 As Hayao states, 'When hollowness occupies the center, however, that final conflict which determines who should play the central role in this integration can be avoided. This model permits the coexistence of opposing forces.' Kumakura, 'The Culture': 5.

In the realm of the contemporary world, what does 'hollow centre' or even the notion of emptiness mean? In a chapter on the subject of silence[18] I suggested that it has many attributes, among them notions of silence inhabiting among other elements, two conditions: the diachronic and the synchronic ... time in motion, and time of the immediate.

Reinforcing the notion of the diachronic, film suggests moments of the hollow centre ... tensions between varying forces ... of life and death, in the case of Bergman's *The Seventh Seal*. In the film the protagonist, a knight returning from one of the Crusades is confronted with a ghostly figure who challenges him to a duel ... a game of chess. In the end the knight discovers who his challenger is ... in of all places, a confessor's chamber of the Church. The challenger is of course, death itself. This moment of confrontation between the knight and death is one that suggests a definition of the 'hollow centre' for me. It is that centre between two systems that Bergman himself was confronted with ... belief in something called the divine, versus the knight who observes that: 'life is an outrageous horror ... knowing that all is nothingness.'[19] Here, however, unlike the 'hollow centre' found in Japanese culture, there really is no equilibrium. Hence, the existentialist conditions that Kierkegaard, Dostoyevsky, Nietzsche, and Sartre all confronted themselves with, following a similar pursuit,. ... the potentiality of a non-existent god.[20] Therefore, wherein lies happiness? Does it even exist in Bergman's world?

Dao and Other Matters

> Don't listen with your ears, listen with your mind. No, don't listen with your mind, but listen with your spirit. Listening stops with the ears, the mind stops with recognition, but spirit is empty and waits on all things. The Way gathers in emptiness alone. Emptiness is the fasting of the Mind.[21]

In a manner similar to the dialogues between Socrates and his audience, but certainly quite different philosophically, Confucius conveys to a student his observations and advocates a meditational process of emptying the mind

---

18 Robert Hermanson, 'Multiple Silences in a Cacophonous Age,' (paper presented at the 1st Global Conference: 'Exploring and Managing Silence,' Mansfield College, Oxford, UK, July 6–8, 2015).
19 Hermanson, 'Multiple Silences'
20 Hermanson, 'Multiple Silences'
21 Chuang Tzu, *The Complete Works of Chuang Tzu*, trans. Burton Watson, (New York: Columbia University Press, 1968), 57–58.

and making oneself receptive to the Way. The Way or *Dao* has three primary meanings: it is understood as the ontological source of creation, the process of constant change that characterizes the created world, and the path of human action that can align individuals with this overarching cosmic process.[22] But what human action is required to achieve this in light of the fact that humankind has long been dominated by chaos, suffering, absurdities?

For Chuang Tzu (Zhuangzi) the answer was to free oneself from the world through the notion of the wanderer. That the notion of the wanderer can be observed as another aspect of the Chuang Tzu, namely that called *Wu-wei* (literally 'non-action') is one of the most intriguing and confounding elements of Daoist thought. Through a mastery of 'action-less actions' people can through the development of their own skills and artistries, act almost instinctively and spontaneously, and yet achieve a form of success, and presumably, happiness. Hence, it remains an enigma.

Are there wanderers in the present *zeitgeist* in a similar pursuit of happiness? Curiously, not that long ago, the notion of the *flâneur* emerged in the bohemian world of Paris and the *Belle Époque* era. A western construct, in contrast to the *Wu-wei*, the *flâneur* could stroll the streets of the modern metropolis, and, as Baudelaire once observed: 'be at the centre of the world, and yet to remain hidden from the world ... a prince who everywhere rejoices in his incognito.'[23] Yet, even in the present post-modern world the notion of the *flâneur* also suggests modern alienation, mass culture and the spectatorial gaze.[24] ... but in pursuit of what?

4   Fullness or Emptiness in the Pursuit of Happiness?

Within the present *zeitgeist* can both fullness and emptiness exist as means by which happiness can be achieved? On one hand, I would argue that the

---

22   New World Encyclopedia contributors, 'Zhuangzi,' *New World Encyclopedia*, viewed 14 January 2016, http://www.newworldencyclopedia.org/p/index.php?title=Zhuangzi&oldid=795345

23   Charles Baudelaire, *The Painter of Modern Life and Other Essays*, trans. Jonathan Mayne, (New York: Phaidon Press, 1964), 9.

24   'The discourse of visibility prioritized by consumerism, that is, the primacy of the acts of looking and being looked at which are central to media texts, highlights the ways in which the power relationships of consumer culture are organized around the idea of the gaze. Who looks? Who and what is looked at?,' Mehita Iqani, *Consumer Culture and the Media: Magazines in the Public Eye* (New York: Palgrave Macmillan, St. Martins Press LLC, 2012), 34.

modern world is already filled with 'stuff' ... possessions of wealth, prosperity, successes that convey the elusive 'pursuit of happiness' a term that so moved the founding fathers to include the phrase in the United States Declaration of Independence. Our consumer driven world, filled with excesses, only attempts to achieve even more. But what has fullness really achieved?

On the other hand, an attempt at the removal of 'stuff' from our lives, has been experimented with through Zen meditations, yoga exercises, experiments with hallucinogenic experiences. For many, also meaningful spiritual retreats ... all in an effort to remove ourselves from the cacophonous world we are surrounded by. In my chapter on silence, previously referred to and in response to a profound commentary by Max Picard on the loss of silence, I observed that there are multiple silences that exist including the rhetorical, and ultimately, the silence of the self.[25] Within this world of the self and removed from such cacophonies, are we finally able to reach some kind of Nirvana?

Is happiness therefore a quest, a desire, a need for something beyond ourselves, that is only to be pursued as a future goal? And if so, how will we know when we have arrived? Therefore, is it merely an illusion? Or. ... is it also something more immediate, a kind of serendipitous moment in our lives in which we can find an internal satisfaction, as well as a shared warmth ... as comforting, perhaps, as a warm puppy? The enigmatic answer I would suggest, remains within our own true selves.

Bibliography

Baudelaire, Charles. *The Painter of Modern Life and Other Essays*. Translated by Jonathan Mayne. New York: Phaidon Press, 1964.

Chuang Tzu. *The Complete Works of Chuang Tzu*. Translated by Burton Watson. New York: Columbia University Press, 1968.

Hara, Kenya. *White*. Translated by Jooyeon Rhee, Zurich: Lars Müller, 2009. Viewed 25 January, 2016, http://www.amazon.com/White-Kenya-Hara/dp3037781831\.

Hermanson, Robert. 'Secularization vs. Sacralization: The Paradoxical City.' Paper presented at the Seventh Savannah Symposium: 'Spirituality of Place,' Savannah, GA, February 17–19, 2011.

Hermanson, Robert. 'Multiple Silences in a Cacophonous Age.' Paper presented at the 1st Global Conference: 'Exploring and Managing Silence.' Mansfield College, Oxford, UK, July 6–8, 2015.

---

25   Hermanson, 'Multiple Silences.'

Iqani, Mehita. *Consumer Culture and the Media: Magazines in the Public Eye*. New York: Palgrave Macmillan, St. Martins Press LLC, 2012.

Kumakura, Isao. 'The Culture of Ma,' *Japan Echo*, 34:1, 2007. Viewed 31 July, 2015, http://www.japanecho.com/sum/2007/340114.html.

Nitschke, Gunter. 'Ma: Place, Space, Void,' *Kyoto Journal* 8, 1988. Viewed January 10, 2016, http://www.kyotojournal.org/the-journal/culture-arts/ma-place-void/.

Osho. *Everyday Osho: 365 Daily Meditations for the Here and Now*. Gloucester, MA.: Fair Winds Press, 2002.

Schulz, Charles M. *Happiness is a Warm Puppy*. Kennebunkport, Maine: Cider Mill Press, 2015.

Spitzer, S.J., Robert. 'The Four Levels of Happiness,' Catholic Education Research Center, Bellevue WA, 1999. Viewed 25 January 2016. http://www.catholiceducation.org/en/religion-and-philosophy/apologetics/the-four-levels-of happiness.html.

Treib, Marc, and Mark Herman. 'Ry-oanji' *A Guide to the Gardens of Kyoto*, 93–95. New York: Kodansha America, Inc., 2003.

Van Leeuwen, Thomas A. P. *The Skyward Trend of Thought*. Cambridge, MA: MIT Press, 1988.

CHAPTER 12

Earthly Happiness and Heavenly Happiness

Seán Moran

Abstract

In this chapter, I endorse the virtues as a route to happiness. I compare the virtues advocated by the ancient Greek philosopher Aristotle with those favoured by the mediaeval theologian Thomas Aquinas, and then use a modified argument of the enlightenment mathematician and philosopher Blaise Pascal to arrive at a rational position. To be happy is to flourish, Aristotle claims. This is an objective condition, and not the same as a fleeting feeling of subjective wellbeing. As he famously puts it: 'One swallow does not make a summer' (1098a18-20).[1] For Aristotle, the flourishing life is one lived in accordance with the virtues. These are stable dispositions – such as justice, courage and practical wisdom – that enable a person to live a good life. However, to Aquinas, the virtuous life is not an end in itself, but merely a preparation for the after-life. The type of happiness that awaits us then is much superior to mundane flourishing. Aquinas believes that there is *felicitas* (the ordinary, earthly happiness that Aristotle analyses) and there is heavenly happiness or *beatitudo perfecta*. If Aristotle is correct, it's reasonable for anyone to desire being animated by the virtues and hence to attain an enduring happiness: 'the best, noblest, and most pleasant thing in the world' (1099a).[2] But Aquinas's extended view would only seem plausible to theists, and merely to a proportion of these, at best. Pascal offers the (highly contestable) argument that it is rational to believe in God, since the potential rewards outweigh any minor encumbrances of such conviction. I consider an adapted version of 'Pascal's Wager' to explore whether Aquinas's virtues have a more general application. I finally conjecture that a judiciously selected range of virtues can still conduce to earthly happiness, with the potential bonus of heavenly happiness (if such a possibility exists).

Keywords

happiness – Aristotle – Aquinas – flourishing – *felicitas* – *beatitudo perfecta* – Pascal's wager – afterlife

---

1 Aristotle, *Nicomachean Ethics*, trans. James A.K. Thompson (London: Penguin Books, 2004).
2 Ibid.

1   Introduction

Is everybody happy? I hope so. We all want to be happy; of course we do. Aristotle says that 'Happiness ... is the best, noblest, and most pleasant thing in the world' (1099a).[3] Who would not want to be happy? The American *Declaration of Independence* of 4 July 1776 apparently guarantees the right to 'life, liberty and the pursuit of happiness'. In the small Himalayan country of Bhutan, they talk about Gross National Happiness. And 100 years ago, in its *Proclamation of Independence*, the Irish Republic 'declares its resolve to pursue the happiness and prosperity of the whole nation'.

2   Subjective Wellbeing

But characterizing happiness is a different matter; and measuring it is even harder. One prominent writer on happiness – Richard Layard – defines it as 'feeling good – enjoying life and feeling it is wonderful'.[4] This initially sounds like a reasonable definition, but perhaps it is a tad crude. A little unsophisticated, too, is his approach of simply asking people if they are happy (like I did at the start of my talk in Budapest).

However, Layard's work has attracted quite a bit of interest, particularly since it is now being used to make international comparisons. The *2015 World Happiness Report* attempts to quantify the 'Subjective Wellbeing' (SWB) of various nations.[5] The happiest country in the world is now ... Switzerland. It must be the chocolate and the yodeling. The Nordic countries, plus Australia and New Zealand are up there too. And the least happy (at number 158) is the Republic of Togo (on the coast of sub-Saharan Africa, near Ghana and the Ivory Coast), with Syria and Afghanistan similarly miserable. Bhutan is mid-table at 79. But my own country, Ireland, is rated number 18 in the world for happiness. Americans do even better, at 15. Our present location, Hungary, is placed at 104, however, so we should do our best to cheer people up while we are here for this conference.

Although these figures are interesting, there are certain problems with Layard's general approach. One difficulty is that each person's happiness goes up and down during the day (a feature that Layard himself recognizes). We

---

3   Ibid.
4   Richard Layard, 'The Secrets of Happiness', *New Statesman*, 3 March 2003, 25.
5   John F. Helliwell, Richard Layard and Jeffrey Sachs, eds., *World Happiness Report 2015* (New York: Sustainable Development Solutions Network, 2015).

might thus treat these survey results with caution. And because people mean different things by the word 'happiness', Layard only tries to measure *Subjective Well Being*. He asks them questions such as: 'would you say you are very happy, pretty happy or not too happy?'[6] This relies on people self-reporting how they are feeling. It is not so different from singing the children's song to them: 'If you're happy and you know it, clap your hands'.

However they could be wrong about their own happiness. They might be happy and not know it; or unhappy and not know it. He is relying on them being 'Happy and you know it, and you really want to show it'. I suggest that the epistemology is problematic and that the research participants could be wrong. This sounds slightly strange: how can people be in error about themselves? Surely they have privileged access to their own states of mind? Well perhaps they do have some access – though that's debatable – but it does not render people's happiness transparent to themselves. Let me explain by giving an example. Were Layard to ask a heroin addict of my acquaintance if he was happy, he might say 'Yes' (depending on the time of day). But if we were to observe the unfortunate fellow over a period of time, we would have to say 'No'. His life of opiate addiction is not a happy life. And if the addict thinks that he is happy, he's simply mistaken. His subjective and objective happiness have become decoupled.

3 Objective Wellbeing in Aristotle

A different way of thinking about happiness is to replace the idea of Subjective Well Being – an elusive quality – with something more rational. *Objective Well Being*, we might call it. This is what Aristotle does. Furthermore, he feels that we can only decide if a person is happy by considering 'a complete lifetime' (1098a20-21).[7] Aristotle famously says that: 'One swallow does not make a summer [...] Similarly neither can one day ... make a man blessed and happy' (Ibid.). So what does make a person happy over the longer term? What is the Good Life?

There is some ambiguity in Aristotle's answer. In Book 10 of the *Nicomachean Ethics* he elevates the life of contemplation (the *bios theoretikos*) to one of perfect flourishing. At 1170a16, Aristotle tells us that *theoria* is the 'most divine element in us'. Contemplation is the highest operation for this activity enables

---

[6] Layard, 'Secrets of Happiness', 25.
[7] Aristotle, *Nicomachean Ethics*.

us to 'understand noble and divine things' (1177a10-20).[8] But he has devoted the previous nine books largely to extolling the benefits of the civic life and of friendship. And he suggests that the life of contemplation would be 'too high for man' (1177b).[9]

So Aristotle offers a duplex thesis about happiness rather than a unified account. We should use some solitary leisure time to think about lofty things. But we should also enjoy the company of our friends and the everyday life of the *polis*. This sounds like the academic life, doesn't it? Some of us in this conference room must be happy and flourishing, in that case. Are we?

And in everything we do, according to Aristotle, we should aim for a 'happy medium'. Not too much; not too little; just the right amount: like Goldilocks in the children's story. That is Aristotle's recipe for the Good Life, the happy life. So our unfortunate heroin addict does not live a good life, but one that is severely out of balance. And if he tells us that he is happy, he is objectively wrong. He is simply not flourishing.

Aristotle is very clear about the superiority of a moderate, rational life over base existence and decadent excess (1095b15-20).[10] The rock star lifestyle would hold no appeal for him. In fact, he talks of the 'bovine' life of pleasure as being not properly human. Such unfavourable animal comparisons are quite common in this area. Plato says that the hedonist lives the 'life of a mollusc' (21d),[11] and the Victorian writer Thomas Carlyle calls hedonism 'the philosophy of swine'.[12] Nor are wealth, power or glory the way to achieve happiness.

In fact, Aristotle defines his version of happiness, *eudaimonia*, as 'activity of the soul in accordance with virtue'. Activity in accordance with virtue? This doesn't sound very much like happiness. But Aristotle does not of course intend the word 'virtuous' in the thin-lipped, prim and boring Victorian sense. Nor would his construal match the *Old Testament* notion of a 'virtuous woman' (Proverbs 31:10).[13] On the contrary, he means that we should live a life of courage; a life of justice; a live of practical wisdom; a life of temperance. This is the 'paradox of hedonism': that pleasure is most effectively pursued indirectly.

8   Ibid.
9   Ibid.
10 Ibid.
11 Plato, *Philebus*, Edith Hamilton & Huntington Cairns, eds., *Plato: Collected Dialogues*, Nineteenth Printing (Princeton: Princeton University Press, 2005).
12 Roger Crisp, 'Well-Being', *The Stanford Encyclopedia of Philosophy*, Summer 2015 Edition, Edward N. Zalta, ed., (Stanford: Stanford University Press, 2015), viewed 10 April 2016, http://plato.stanford.edu/archives/sum2015/entries/well-being/.
13 Robert Carroll, ed., *The Bible*, Authorized King James Version (Oxford: Oxford World Classics, 2008).

And the best indirect means are the virtues, which can lead us to joy. Virtue is its own reward, and we are to rejoice when our virtues animate us. In fact, 'The man who does not rejoice in noble actions is not even good ...', according to Aristotle (1099a).[14] As well as the four 'cardinal virtues' (not a term that Aristotle uses) of courage, justice, temperance and practical wisdom, he lists a variety of other moral and intellectual virtues – including the delightful disposition of *eutrapelia* (wittiness: the mean between boorishness and buffoonery).

4 Aquinas's Development of Aristotle's Theory

Sixteen centuries after Aristotle, the philosopher and theologian Thomas Aquinas develops his theory of happiness. He believes that four Greek virtues are needed for earthly happiness: courage, justice, wisdom and temperance. These are also in the *Old Testament* deuterocanonical Book of Wisdom (8:7),[15] so he has some biblical reason for endorsing them in addition to his respect for Aristotle (whom he calls 'The Philosopher'). But Aquinas takes the view that only a lesser happiness – *felicitas* – is possible during our time on earth if we are animated by the four cardinal virtues.

To Aquinas, true happiness (*beatitudo perfecta*) is only available in the afterlife. Aquinas believes that three more important virtues are needed to attain such heavenly happiness. These are the theological virtues of faith, hope and charity. Here he departs from Aristotle's analysis, which goes no further than earthly flourishing. A blissful hereafter is our ultimate *telos* or end, for 'there can be no complete and final happiness for us save in the vision of God (*visio beatifica*)' (1a2æ, q.3, a.8).[16] This beatific vision is direct and unmediated knowledge of God's presence: not reflected 'in a glass darkly' (1 Corinthians 13:12),[17] but in complete and loving *perichoretic* union with the Trinity. At this point, we will be both subjectively and objectively happy. We will be ecstatic, in fact.

It is hard to know what else awaits us in the afterlife. Biblical guidance is sketchy, but the dress code seems to be white linen. White suits? It will be like the 1970s all over again: John Travolta in *Saturday Night Fever*. On the upside,

---

14   Aristotle, *Nicomachean Ethics*.
15   Carroll, ed., *Bible*.
16   Thomas Aquinas, *Summa Theologica*, tr. Fathers of the English Dominican Province, (New York: Benziger Bros., 1947), viewed 2 April 2016, http://www.ccel.org/ccel/aquinas/summa.html.
17   Carroll, ed., *Bible*.

there will be no hunger, thirst or sunstroke, but plenty of incense and angels. The golden city of the New Jerusalem, with its gates, rivers and precious stones sounds wonderful. Technicolor bling. But I'm not too sure about the music. Trumpets and harps? Just imagine that sound for a moment: trumpet and harp. It doesn't work.

The Muslim vision of paradise is more detailed. Qur'anic exegesis and tradition (*Hadīth*) point to some interesting features about paradise. I am pleased to read, for example, that only 66 percent of the places in paradise are reserved for Muslims.[18] There is room then for non-Muslims. Every person there will speak the language of Muhammad, and be the age of Jesus (33 years).[19] It will be excellent to be 33 again but my Arabic is terrible, so I hope that we are given fluency as a divine gift. Various sources also give particulars of the physical pleasures that await us there, but perhaps I had better not go into too much detail about these. Muslim scholars in Pakistan and the United Arab Emirates, with whom I have had discussions recently, explained that they are only metaphorical anyway. However, as a flute-player, I am happy that there will apparently be flutes in paradise. But, best of all is the promise – identical to the Christian promise – that the blessed will enjoy the beatific vision.[20] We will experience the supreme bliss and happiness of seeing the Face of God, 'the most pleasurable of all paradisical delights'.[21] A cherub will lift the veil from God's face, which will illuminate our own faces by the light of truth.

(Come to think of it, the flutes would go well with the harps. If we could do a swap with the brass players in the Christian heaven and transfer a few flautists across, that would make for much better ensemble playing. There would be no problem persuading typical brass players to enter the Islamic paradise: the promise of unlimited drink and food would be enough. And they might even be tempted by the other delights ... after they had drunk and eaten to excess.)

Of course, theologians will tell us that the transcendental bliss of paradise is beyond our imagination, and that the images we have are merely allegorical. Nevertheless, being in the divine presence and enjoying the beatific vision sounds like an attractive prospect. But such a promise is only plausible to some theists.

---

18 Aziz al-Azmeh, 'Rhetoric for the Senses: A Consideration of Muslim Paradise Narratives', *Journal of Arabic Literature*, 26.3 (1995): 218.
19 Ibid., 223.
20 Ibid., 218.
21 Ibid., 228.

5 A Rational Approach

What then is a rational approach towards the virtues? If Aristotle is correct, it is reasonable for everyone to desire being animated by the virtues and hence to attain an enduring happiness or *eudaimonia*: 'the best, noblest, and most pleasant thing in the world'. The virtues don't just lead to flourishing: they actually constitute flourishing. So we ought to live a temperate life of courage and justice, regulated by practical wisdom, and involving a range of other virtues. We should develop these by engaging in some solitary contemplation, and by spending time with friends and fellow citizens. The virtues conduce to – and embody – a purely earthly happiness that is available (in principle) to all humans.

If Aquinas is correct, we should still cultivate Aristotle's earthly virtues, in order to enjoy *felicitas* in this life. But some modifications will be needed. For example, the dispositions of pride and humility change their status as we move from Aristotle to Aquinas. As far as the ancient Greeks are concerned, pride is a virtue and humility is a vice. But the Christian analysis is virtually the inverse of this: humility is a virtue and pride is a vice. The good person is humble not proud, for pride is the cause of all the other sins, according to Aquinas. And to enjoy the beatific vision in paradise, we should also be motivated by faith, hope and charity. The crucial question here though is: What if Aquinas is wrong?

The enlightenment mathematician and philosopher Blaise Pascal can help us to arrive at a rational position. Pascal's Wager, in essence, offers the argument that belief in God is rational, since the potential rewards outweigh any minor encumbrances of such conviction. Having 'weighed the gain and loss', Pascal suggests that we 'wager that He [God] is'.[22] Joseph Ratzinger summarises the advice that Pascal gives to his atheist friends. He recommends that those who do not 'succeed in finding the way of accepting God, should, nevertheless, seek to live and to direct his life *"veluti si Deus daretur"*, as if God existed'.[23]

If, for the sake of argument, we accept Pascal's analysis, what are the potential benefits and what are the possible drawbacks? The advantages are clear: heavenly bliss; the beatific vision; food; drink; music. And the disadvantages? We should not be proud and arrogant, but humble and gentle. Some of my colleagues in management positions would find this difficult, but it should be achievable by decent human beings. Similarly, we could be a bit more charitable to our fellow men and women: a little more benevolent. This would not

---

22 Blaise Pascal, *Pensées*, tr. W.F. Trotter (New York: P.F. Collier, 1910): §233.
23 In Joel Hodge, 'From desire to conversion: Pascal's wager and Girard's mimetic theory', *The Heythrop Journal*, 56.6 (2014): 7.

be too big a sacrifice. And even if the afterlife turns out to be an illusion, the everyday world would be a better place with less arrogance and more benevolence.

If the disposition to be charitable is widely valued by atheists, agnostics and believers alike, perhaps the sticking points are the other two theological virtues: faith and hope. According to Aquinas, though, these are not virtues that we have to cultivate ourselves, but will be given to us supernaturally if we permit such a thing.

6 Conclusion

Aristotle and Aquinas are united in the belief that earthly flourishing (*eudaimonia* or *felicitas*: Greek or Latin) arises from the natural virtues (courage, justice and so on). We can perhaps accept that such virtues are beneficial to this life, and concede that it is reasonable to cultivate them. But, our corollary of Pascal's wager suggests that it is also rational to be charitable and to show humility – including the intellectual humility of open-mindedness. These extra virtues might open the door to paradise. But if they don't, nothing much has been lost. In fact, we will have gained something, for virtue is reputedly its own reward.

In finishing, I can do no better than to quote the Scottish poet, Robert Burns in his epitaph 'On a Friend', written in 1784:

> An honest man here lies at rest, [...]
> The friend of man, the friend of truth,
> The friend of age, and guide of youth:
> Few hearts like his, with virtue warm'd,
> Few heads with knowledge so inform'd;
> If there's another world, he lives in bliss;
> If there is none, he made the best of this.[24]

Bibliography

al-Azmeh, Aziz. 'Rhetoric for the Senses: A Consideration of Muslim Paradise Narratives'. *Journal of Arabic Literature* 26.3 (1995): 215–231.

---

24 Robert Burns, *The Collected Poems of Robert Burns: With an Introduction and Bibliography* (Ware: Wordsworth Edition, 1994): 286.

Aquinas, Thomas. *Summa Theologica*. Translated by the Fathers of the English Dominican Province. New York: Benziger Bros., 1947. Viewed 2 April 2016. http://www.ccel.org/ccel/aquinas/summa.html.

Burns, Robert. *The Collected Poems of Robert Burns: With an Introduction and Bibliography*. Ware: Wordsworth Edition, 1994.

Carroll, Robert, ed. *The Bible: Authorized King James Version*. Oxford: Oxford World Classics, 2008.

Crisp, Roger. 'Well-Being'. *The Stanford Encyclopedia of Philosophy*. Summer 2015 Edition. Edited by Edward N. Zalta. Stanford: Stanford University Press, 2015. Viewed 10 April 2016. http://plato.stanford.edu/archives/sum2015/entries/well-being/.

Helliwell, John F., Richard Layard and Jeffrey Sachs, eds. *World Happiness Report 2015*. New York: Sustainable Development Solutions Network, 2015.

Hodge, Joel. 'From desire to conversion: Pascal's wager and Girard's mimetic theory'. *The Heythrop Journal*, 56.6 (2014): 1–12.

Layard, Richard. 'The Secrets of Happiness'. *New Statesman*, 3 March 2003.

Pascal, Blaise. *Pensées* Translated by W.F. Trotter. New York: P.F. Collier, 1910.

CHAPTER 13

Happiness in Higher Education in Hong Kong: an Anthropology Study

Kelly K. L. Chan

Abstract

Since the transfer of sovereignty from the United Kingdom to China took place in 1997, Hong Kong has been going through an identity crisis, questioning Beijing's sincerity in maintaining its wellbeing. In recent years, there has also been a continuous decline in the level of happiness in Hong Kong. Among the 158 countries and territories assessed, Hong Kong ranked 75th in 2016,[1] down from 72nd in 2015,[2] 64th in 2013,[3] and 46th in 2012[4] in the World Happiness Report. However, statistical comparison of happiness is not enough, empirical cross-cultural research on happiness or wellbeing fails to identify and explain the nature of happiness and the different ways of 'being well'.[5] From the anthropology perspective, humans do not have *one* single 'pursuit of happiness'.[6] Nonetheless, socio-cultural anthropology has been institutionally averse to the study of happiness;[7] and there is very little understanding of what constitutes happiness in

---

1   John Helliwell, Richard Layard and Jeffery Sachs, *World Happiness Report 2016, Update, Vol. I* (New York: Sustainable Development Solutions Network, 2016), 21.
2   Helliwell, Layard and Sachs, *World Happiness Report 2015*, 27.
3   Helliwell, Layard and Sachs, *World Happiness Report 2013*, 23.
4   Helliwell, Layard and Sachs, *World Happiness Report*, 44.
5   Shinobu Kitayama and Hazel Rose Markus, 'The Pursuit of Happiness and the Realization of Sympathy: Cultural Patterns of Self, Social Relations, and Well-Being', *Culture and Subjective Well-Being*, eds. Ed Diener and Eunkook M. Shu (Cambridge, MA: MIT Press, 2000): 113–161; Gordon Mathews, 'Happiness Culture and Context', *International Journal of Wellbeing* 2.4 (2012): 299–312.
6   Gordon Mathews and Carolina Izquierdo, *Pursuits of Happiness: Well-Being in Anthropological Perspective* (New York: Berghahn Books, 2009), 5.
7   Neil Thin, 'Happiness and the Sad Topics of Anthropology', (University of Bath: Wellbeing in Developing Countries Working Paper No. 10, WeD – Wellbeing in Developing Countries ESRC Research Group, 2005); Neil Thin, *Social Happiness: Research into Policy and Practice* (Bristol: Policy Press, 2012).

the context of education, one exception being the work of Noddings.[8] The inattention to 'happiness' in education studies, policies and evaluations fails to consider either the happiness of students or the contribution of education to lifelong happiness. This anthropological study is interested in how university students define 'happiness', and how happiness is constituted and experienced in the context of higher education. The study started in January 2016 and is currently being carried out in Hong Kong. Rather than numbers, this study asks: 1. What 'happiness' means in a higher education context in Hong Kong; 2. How 'happiness' is expressed and experienced in the higher education institutes; and 3. How 'happiness' relates to learning.

Keywords

happiness – wellbeing – higher education – anthropology – visual ethnography – Hong Kong

1   Introduction

Since the transfer of sovereignty over Hong Kong from the United Kingdom to China in 1997, the education system in Hong Kong has undergone a series of changes. The already keen competition for higher education has intensified as students from all over China compete for places in Hong Kong universities. While the overall education level of the Hong Kong population has increased over the last 5 years, the higher educational level, however, has not made Hong Kong a happier place. The World Happiness Report has shown a continuous reduced level of happiness in Hong Kong since 2012. Also, the annual Hong Kong Happiness Index Survey conducted by Lingnan University revealed the latest Happiness Index in 2015 at 70.0 (out of 100), the lowest since 2009.[9] Moreover, Lingnan's survey in 2011 reported that 'education reduces happiness'.[10] Educationalist Noddings, however, insists that happiness ought to be an aim of education, and 'a good education should contribute

---

8   Nel Noddings, *Happiness and Education* (Cambridge: Cambridge University Press, 2003).
9   'Happiness Index', *Centre for Public Policy Studies* (Hong Kong: Lingnan University, 2015), viewed 18 April 2016, https://www.ln.edu.hk/cpps/08_highlight/08-happiness.html.
10   The 'ING LIFE Happiness Survey' attempted to find out how levels of education related to happiness. Over 8,500 Hong Kong residents volunteered to take the online survey and responded to questions divided into four categories: Love, Insight, Fortitude and

significantly to personal and collective happiness'.[11] Happiness and its relationship to 'a good education' and learning in general is, therefore, worthy of scholarly research.

A (Un)Happiness and Education in Hong Kong

Since 1997, Hong Kong has been governed under the 'One country, two systems' constitutional policy. The latest survey from the Public Opinion Program of the University of Hong Kong shows Hong Kong's trust in the policy has fallen sharply in the past five years.[12] The positive relationship between trust and happiness has been well demonstrated in literature.[13] The loss in trust in governance and management might have contributed to the reduced level of happiness in recent years. Researchers have attempted to rationalize the negative emotions while the media blame it on the unstable social and political situation. The people in Hong Kong are constantly reminded of how 'sad' they are, as they are regularly exposed to reports like, 'Sad city: Hong Kong comes bottom of Asian happiness survey. The city's score has hit a record low – worse even than during the SARS outbreak',[14] and 'Hong Kong happiness index hits 7-year low'.[15]

In Hong Kong, nine years of compulsory education (including six years primary and 3 years junior secondary) is provided free, with three years senior secondary education freely accessible. Since 1997, there have been changes in the language of instruction policies and also the senior secondary curriculum. The new model of 3+3+4 policy (three years junior secondary, three years of senior secondary then four years of university) was introduced in 2009. The education level of the population of Hong Kong has

---

Engagement (Hong Kong: Lingnan University, 2011), viewed 18 April 2016, https://www.ln.edu.hk/news/20110802/happinessindex2011.

11   Noddings, *Happiness and Education*, 1.

12   'The People's Confidence, in "One Country, Two Systems", *Public Opinion Programme* (The University of Hong Kong, 2016), viewed 18 April 2016, https://www.hkupop.hku.hk/english/popexpress/trust/conocts/.

13   John Helliwell and Shun Wang, 'Trust and Well-Being', *International Journal of Wellbeing*, 1.1 (2011): 42–78, viewed 18 April 2016, www.internationaljournalofwellbeing.org/index.php/ijow/article/view/3/85.

14   Elizabeth Cheung, 'Hong Kong Bottom of Happiness Survey', *South China Morning Post*, 17 February 2015, viewed 18 April 2016, http://www.scmp.com/news/hong-kong/article/1715776/hong-kong-comes-bottom-asian-happiness-survey.

15   'Hong Kong Happiness Index Hits 7-Year Low', *Ejinsight*, 1 December 2015, viewed 18 April 2016, http://www.ejinsight.com/20151201-hong-kong-happiness-index-hits-7-year-low-poll-shows/.

increased over the last 5 years. Nearly 30% of the population aged 15 and over has attained post-secondary educational level in 2014, compared to 26% in 2010.[16]

Currently the number of places available for undergraduate degrees is substantially fewer than the number of students who satisfy the entry requirements for general admission to local universities. In 2015, more than 25,000 local students who fulfilled the entry requirements had to compete for the 15,000 first-year first-degree places in nine government-funded universities and institutes.[17] The lack of university places means that students have to further their education overseas or in sub-degree programmes.

B   *Definitions of Happiness*

The subjectivity of individual experience of emotions makes it problematic to define and measure happiness. Researchers have suggested universal definitions of happiness, such as Veenhoven's definition: 'the degree to which an individual judges the overall quality of his life favourably'.[18] Philosophers who write about 'happiness' typically take it to be either a state of mind (in a psychological sense), or a life that goes well for the person leading it (as in a sense of well-being).[19] Such universal definitions do not take cultural perspectives into consideration. In anthropology, Mathews and Izquierdo give a multifolded definition of happiness as 'well-being':

> an optimal state for an individual, community, society, and the world as a whole. It is conceived of, expressed, and experienced in different ways by different individuals and within the cultural contexts of different societies: different societies may have distinctly different culturally shaped visions of well-being.[20]

This notion of 'well-being' resonates across cultures 'due to our common humanity and interrelatedness over space and time'.[21]

---

16 Factsheets published by the Information Services Department, Hong Kong Special Administrative Region Government, 2015.

17 2,300 out of the 15,000 places were assigned to overseas students, whom are mostly from Mainland China.

18 Ruut Veenhoven, 'Is Happiness Relative', *Social Indicators Research* 24 (1991): 1–34.

19 Dan Haybron, 'Happiness', *The Stanford Encyclopaedia of Philosophy* (Fall 2011), viewed 18 April 2016, http://plato.stanford.edu/archives/fall2011/entries/happiness/.

20 Mathews and Izquierdo, *Pursuits of Happiness*, 5.

21 Mathews and Izquierdo, *Pursuits of Happiness*, 5.

Mathews and Izquiredo explain that 'well-being' is experienced by individuals but it may be considered and compared interpersonally and interculturally, since all individuals live within a society, and all societies live in a common world at large.[22] In this research, I use the term 'happiness' informed by Mathews and Izquierdo's comprehensive definition of 'well-being'. Happiness is intangible. You cannot see, feel, touch or taste it except through the agency of something else. For example, one can feel happy through listening to music, being with another person or through participating in various activities. Happiness could be described as a state of mind, which is expressed in different ways among different people and it has different causes. Taking an ethnographic approach, this research aims to capture the complexities of the intangible. We can experience happiness and we have behavioural indicators to express it. However, our recognition of the indicators might not always be accurate nor would they be universally understood; for instance, a smile could be an expression of joy or simply a social manner and while in some cultures a smile that shows the teeth indicates happiness, in others the teeth would be hidden no matter how joyful someone felt. Hence the importance of understanding the contexts in which happiness is expressed and experienced.

In this study, 'happiness' is a subjective experience of an individual dependent on personal and social factors and often context-bound. In the context of higher education, for example, achievement of a personal goal such as assuming a leadership role in an academic committee or an experience of peer/family support in one's studies may lead to happiness. 'Satisfaction' is a sense of the meeting of expectations. In higher education this depends on whether the university or institution has met the expectation of the students as advertised. The evaluative tool to measure satisfaction adopted by universities is quantitative by nature and therefore raises the question as to whether it can effectively reflect subjective experiences of happiness and provide insight to inform change.

C   *Higher Education as a Cultural Ecology*

Anthropologist Julian Steward coined the term 'cultural ecology' as a methodology for understanding how human beings adapt to such a wide variety

---

22   Culture and society are often confused and have a level of commonality. For the purposes of this research, culture is defined as a system of practices and beliefs that have been passed down overtime and are adhered to by all members and sustained by rituals and artefacts; society can be made up of several cultures and subcultures sharing the same space and linked by common ideas or concerns.

of environments.[23] Gregory Bateson was the first to apply 'cultural ecology' in his project.[24] Bateson considers culture and the human mind as 'open, dynamic systems based on living interrelationships between the mind and the world, and within the mind itself'.[25] To deepen understanding of the perspectives of the members of the culture,[26] in this case, the students, teachers and the management in various institutes, I conceptualise each of these higher education institutes as a cultural ecology that sit within increasingly larger ecologies and are influenced by them in their practices and outputs.

In the society of Hong Kong are a range of belief systems, cultural practices and identities. For the majority of those who are of Chinese origin, Confucian thinking remains a considerable influence and is enacted through rituals and beliefs within family and social systems and institutions. Learning has long been associated with pleasure and happiness as early as the Confucian period. What delighted Confucius was life: learning, exploring, music, ritual, courtesy and respect.[27] Confucius believes everyone who has the determination to learn should be given equal respect. Noddings emphasizes that the education system in a good society will encourage its people 'to explore and appreciate a full range of possibilities for promoting happiness'. Education, by its very nature, is to help people develop their best selves – 'to become people with pleasing talents, useful and satisfying occupations, self-understanding, sound character, a host of appreciations, and a commitment to continuous learning'.[28] This research is interested in how people define happiness, why they pursue higher education, and how happiness is constituted and experienced in the cultural ecology of an institutionalised higher education.

---

23 Julian Haynes Steward, *Theory of Culture Change: The Methodology of Multilinear Evolution* (Urbana and Chicago: University of Illinois Press, 1972).
24 Gregory Bateson, *Steps to an Ecology of Mind* (London: Jason Aaronson Inc., 1973).
25 Hubert Zapf, 'Cultural Ecology, Postmodernism, and Literary Knowledge', *Redefining Modernism and Postmodernism*, eds. Şebnem Toplu and Hubert Zapf (Newcastle: Cambridge Scholars Publishing, 2010), 9.
26 In early day anthropology, the term 'natives' means people who are born in a certain place. Here I use 'members' to mean the natives because 'native' has become derogatory nowadays.
27 George Jochnowitz, *The Blessed Human Race: Essays on Reconsideration* (Maryland: Hamilton Books, 2007), 44.
28 Noddings, *Happiness and Education*, 23.

2 This Study

This research proposes that by understanding happiness from an anthropological perspective, it can begin to be understood in its social and cultural specificities. Anthropological investigations of values and practices in the context of higher education are important because they reflect issues of beliefs and customs that promise or compromise 'progress/ development' of a society, also defined as 'human well-being'.[29] The purpose is to contribute to the growing demand for anthropological studies in happiness,[30] with a focus on the relationship between happiness and learning. The research looks at a university as a cultural ecology, focuses on how the members of this ecology (the stakeholders, the teachers, and particularly the students as transient members) define happiness, how happiness is constituted and experienced in the context of higher education, and how happiness relates to learning. An ethnographic approach is used to deepen understandings of 'happiness' within the context of higher education in Hong Kong, a crossroads of cultural influences and political struggles, and also within the context of competitive global markets shaping the role of universities. The methods of data collection are observation, exploration of artefacts, field notes and capturing videos. The research take place at two higher education institutes in Hong Kong. The findings may have the potential to be of interest to those exploring the role of 'happiness' in job satisfaction, retention as well as a facilitator of high achievement; how those at work or in educational settings arrive at satisfaction and the conditions that need to be in place to ensure that 'happiness/satisfaction' can thrive in these environments for the benefit of the individual, the community and the organisation. An ethnographic film will be produced as part of the report of results.

3 Method

Traditional anthropological fieldwork requires ethnographers to immerse themselves in the culture she is studying, carrying out research 24-7 and

---

29 Robert Edgerton, *Sick Societies: Challenging the Myth of Primitive Harmony* (Ontario: Simon and Schuster, 2010), 1.
30 Melania Calestani, *An Anthropological Journey into Well-Being: Insights from Bolivia* (New York and London: Springer Science & Business Media, 2012); Neil Thin, *Social Happiness: Research into Policy and Practice* (Bristol: Policy Press, 2012); Michael Jackson, *Life within Limits: Well-Being in a World of Want* (Durham and London: Duke University Press, 2011); Mathews and Izquierdo, *Pursuits of Happiness*.

eventually becoming part of the group she is investigating. With the advancement in technology in videography and photography, 'thinking oneself through in the place of another'[31] has become easier. I am already part of the cultural ecologies in which this research takes place but I have never approached my own culture through an anthropological lens. Taking an anthropological approach, the study includes an examination of artefacts (e.g. the mission statements) which each higher education institute uses to invite young people to participate in its educational experience; and the artefacts (e.g. students' evaluation) completed by students to indicate whether the cultural guardians have been successful in their attempts to 'satisfy' students. These evaluations are artefacts created by the institution to monitor the efficacy of its own education delivery and to meet the requirements of the larger ecology of the government through education policies and regulations. Also widely available online is the informal form of student evaluation such as the entries and comments in student blogs and forums. I study these various forms of documentation to see how different practices and beliefs sustain (or not) the cohesion of the cultural ecology. This is significant to clarify whether the practices of the culture are congruent within the particular culture of the university.

A   *Visual Anthropology*

Happiness is not something easily measurable or visible. Instances of positive emotions can be captured through behaviour and human interaction. Using video recording as the method of data collection, it makes these intangible moments more noticeable – we know it when we see it, we know it when it is absent. Video technology captures 'the repeated, fine-grained scrutiny of moments of social life and sociability'[32] to provide not only a complement to the more conventional techniques, but also a profound realignment in the ways in which human activity could be better analysed. Sarah Pink also suggests ethnography should incorporate visual images and technologies. Visual ethnography acknowledges the interwoven-ness of objects, texts, images and technologies in people's everyday lives and identities; and studies not just social practices etc. as texts, but explores how all types of material, intangible, spoken, performed narratives and discourses are interwoven with and made meaningful.[33] By adopting visual ethnography, I hope to 'focus on the

---

31 Jackson, *Life within Limits*, 196.
32 Christian Heath, Jon Hindmarsch and Paul Luff, *Video in Qualitative Research Analysing Social Interaction in Everyday Life* (London: Sage Publications Ltd, 2010), 3.
33 Sarah Pink, *Doing Visual Ethnography,* 3rd ed. (London: Sage Publications Ltd, 2013), 10.

emotions, the sensual, the artistic, and creative elements'[34] that digital media can capture, realistic representations, collected spontaneously and naturally.[35] I also invite the informants to capture moments of their everyday life in videos as part of the documentation in the production of an ethnographic film. This allows collaboration and enables participants to 'co-own' the product.[36] The method offers descriptive and ethnographic accounts of how individual students experience happiness, which might constitute or contrast with collective ones in an institution.

4 Analysis

This study is currently being carried out in Hong Kong. Based on the status of data collected, which is largely descriptive, I plan to do a thematic coding, 'which involves discovering, interpreting and reporting patterns and clusters of meaning within the data'.[37] My approach avoids the quantification bias by creating an account of 'happiness' in a specific context – higher education. Rather than numbers, this research focuses on my observation as a participant (a teacher-researcher) and narratives of the participants (the students, teachers, and stakeholders). As the methods of data collection are observation documented in field notes and videos, and exploration of artefacts, the analyses first focus on how 'happiness' is described and understood by members of a particular higher education institute. This is followed by a thematic analysis that is discussed in relation to the wider literature.

5 Limitations

The primary aim of this research is to give a chance for the members of the cultural ecology of the university to voice their perceptions of 'happiness' in

---

34 Karen O'Reilly, *Key Concepts in Ethnography* (London: Sage Publications Ltd, 2009), 221.
35 Mike Ball and Greg Smith, 'Technologies of Realism? Ethnographic Uses of Photography and Film', *Handbook of Ethnography*, eds. Paul Atkinson, Amanda Coffey, Sara Delamont, John Lofland and Lyn Lofland (London: Sage Publications Ltd, 2001), 302–319.
36 Pink, *Doing Visual Ethnography*, 64–65.
37 Liz Spencer, et. al., 'Analysis: Principles and Processes', *Qualitative Research Practice: A Guide for Social Science Students & Researchers*, 2nd ed., eds. Jane Ritchie, Jane Lewis, Carol McNaughton Nicholls and Rachel Ormston (London: Sage Publications Ltd, 2013), 269–293.

higher education and any links to learning. While this research has been chosen to be sensitive to the understandings of terms and concepts within a culture, certain issues need to be closely examined. At an institutional level, there are issues of whether disclosure may then publicly disadvantage or advantage that institute over another in terms of findings. Moreover, other contingencies, such as using audio recordings and photos, may also arise in contexts relating to production of the ethnographic film.

6 Conclusion

This chapter proposes an anthropology study of happiness in the context of higher education in Hong Kong, a city in transition from a British colony to a Special Administration Region in China. Nineteen year after the transfer of sovereignty, Hong Kong and the education system have undergone a series of changes. Quantitative studies of Hong Kong's happiness have displayed a gloomy picture. This study aims to offer descriptive and ethnographic accounts of how individual students experience happiness, which might constitute or contrast with collective ones within each higher education institute as a cultural ecology that sits in the wider culture of Hong Kong.

Bibliography

Ball, Mike and Greg Smith. 'Technologies of Realism? Ethnographic Uses of Photography and Film'. *Handbook of Ethnography,* edited by P. A. Atkinson, A. Coffey, S. Delamont, L. H. Lofland and J. Lofland, 302–319. London: Sage Publications Ltd, 2001.

Calestani, Melania. *An Anthropological Journey into Well-Being: Insights from Bolivia.* New York and London: Springer Science & Business Media, 2012.

Cheung, Elizabeth 'Hong Kong Bottom of Happiness Survey'. *South China Morning Post,* 17 February 2015. Viewed 18 April 2016. http://www.scmp.com/news/hong-kong/article/1715776/hong-kong-comes-bottom-asian-happiness-survey.

Chiu, Joanna and Toh Han Shih. 'Proof That You Can't Buy Happiness'. *South China Morning Post,* 19 January 2013. Viewed 18 April 2016. http://www.scmp.com/news/hong-kong/article/1131222/singapore-hong-kong-face-happiness-deficit.

Edgerton, Robert. *Challenging the Myth of Primitive Harmony.* Ontario: Simon and Schuster, 2010.

'Happiness Index'. *Centre for Public Policy Studies.* Hong Kong: Lingnan University, 2015. Viewed 18 April 2016. https://www.ln.edu.hk/cpps/08_highlight/08-happiness.html.

Haybron, Dan. 'Happiness'. *The Stanford Encyclopaedia of Philosophy,* edited by Edward N. Zalta. Fall 2011. Viewed 18 April 2016. http://plato.stanford.edu/archives/fall2011/entries/happiness/.

Heath, Christian, Jon Hindmarsh and Paul Luff. *Video in Qualitative Research Analysing Social Interaction in Everyday Life.* London: Sage Publications, 2010.

Helliwell, John, and Shun Wang. 'Trust and Well-Being'. *International Journal of Wellbeing* 1.1 (2001): 42–78. Viewed 18 April 2016. www.internationaljournalofwellbeing.org/index.php/ijow/article/view/3/85.

Helliwell, John, Richard Layard and Jeffery Sachs. *World Happiness Report 2016, Update, Volume I.* New York: Sustainable Development Solutions Network, 2016.

Helliwell, John, Richard Layard and Jeffery Sachs. *World Happiness Report 2015.* New York: Sustainable Development Solutions Network, 2015.

Helliwell, John, Richard Layard and Jeffery Sachs. *World Happiness Report 2013.* New York: Sustainable Development Solutions Network, 2013.

Helliwell, John, Richard Layard and Jeffery Sachs. *World Happiness Report.* New York: Sustainable Development Solutions Network, 2012.

'Hong Kong Happiness Index Hits 7-Year Low'. *Ejinsight,* 1 December 2015. Viewed 18 April 2016. http://www.ejinsight.com/20151201-hong-kong-happiness-index-hits-7-year-low-poll-shows/.

Jackson, Michael. *Life within Limits: Well-Being in a World of Want.* Durham and London: Duke University Press, 2011.

Jochnowitz, George. *The Blessed Human Race: Essays on Reconsideration.* Maryland: Hamilton Books, 2007.

Kitayama, Shinobu, and Hazel Rose Markus. 'The Pursuit of Happiness and the Realization of Sympathy: Cultural Patterns of Self, Social Relations, and Well-Being'. *Culture and Subjective Well-Being,* edited by Ed Diener and Eunkook M. Suh. 113–161. Cambridge, MA: MIT Press, 2000.

Mathews, Gordon and Carolina Izquierdo. *Pursuits of Happiness: Well-Being in Anthropological Perspective.* New York: Berghahn Books, 2009.

Mathews, Gordon. 'Happiness Culture and Context'. *International Journal of Wellbeing* 2.4 (2012): 299–312.

Noddings, Nel. *Happiness and Education.* Cambridge: Cambridge University Press, 2003.

O'Reilly, Karen. *Key Concepts in Ethnography.* London: Sage Publications Ltd, 2009.

Pink, Sarah. *Doing Visual Ethnography.* London: Sage Publications, 2013.

Spencer L., J. Ritchie, R. Ormston, W. O'Connor and M. Barnard. 'Analysis: Principles and Processes'. *Qualitative Research Practice: A Guide for Social Science Students and Researchers.* 2nd edition, edited by Jane Ritchie, Jane Lewis, Carol McNaughton Nicholls and Rachel Ormston, 269–293. London: SAGE Publications Ltd, 2013.

Steward, Julian Haynes. *Theory of Culture Change: The Methodology of Multilinear Evolution.* Urbana and Chicago: University of Illinois Press, 1972.

'The ING LIFE Happiness Survey'. Hong Kong: Lingnan University, 2011. Viewed 18 April 2016. https://www.ln.edu.hk/news/20110802/happinessindex2011.

'The People's Confidence in "One Country, Two Systems" '. *Public Opinion Programme*. The University of Hong Kong, 2016. Viewed 18 April 2016. https://www.hkupop.hku.hk/english/popexpress/trust/conocts/.

Thin, Neil. *Happiness and the Sad Topics of Anthropology*. Wellbeing in Developing Countries Working Paper No.10. University of Bath: Wellbeing in Developing Countries ESRC Research Group, 2005.

Thin, Neil. *Social Happiness: Research into Policy and Practice*. Bristol: Policy Press, 2012.

Veenhoven, Ruut. 'Is Happiness Relative?' *Social Indicators Research* 24 (1991): 1–34.

Zapf, Hubert. 'Cultural Ecology, Postmodernism, and Literary Knowledge'. *Redefining Modernism and Postmodernism*, edited by Şebnem Toplu and Hubert Zapf, 2–14. Newcastle: Cambridge Scholars Publishing, 2010.

CHAPTER 14

Re-Embracing Simplicity: an Exploration of Epicurean Happiness

Julia Hotz

Abstract

The term 'epicurean' officially dates back to the 12th century A.D, about 1400 years after the death of Epicurus (341-270 B.C) —the ancient Greek philosopher who inspired it.[1] According to today's definition, 'epicurean' means 'fond of or adapted to luxury or indulgence in sensual pleasures'.[2] Such can be confirmed by a simple Google Image search, which associates 'epicurean' with advertisements for extravagant cruise vacations, images of elegant meat and cheese spreads, and other caricatures of luxury. Yet a deeper investigation into the life of Epicurus reveals how the philosopher's core tenets explicitly oppose luxury and indulgence. To quite the contrary, Epicurus' conception of happiness might best be characterized by simplicity—pleasure through primitive, non-material means, like friendship and conversation. By thoroughly exploring the development of Epicurus' philosophy during his lifetime and after his death, this chapter both investigates how 'epicurean' happiness became distorted and considers why forms of *true* epicurean happiness are re-emerging today.

Keywords

epicurus – epicurean – hedonism – *kenodoxia* – *ataraxia* – *aponia* – voluntary simplicity – self-sufficiency

1   The Life and Times of Epicurus

Born 341 B.C on the Greek island of Samos, Epicurus, even in his youth, was doubtful of the supernatural. Perhaps the philosopher's earliest suspicions

---

1   'Epicurean', *Dictionary.com,* accessed on 20 April 2016, http://www.dictionary.com/browse.epicurean.
2   'Epicurean', *Dictionary.com.*

arose from witnessing his mother practice 'folk-healing' as a means of curing illnesses.[3] Similar scepticism surfaced at school, where Epicurus' instructor, the Platonist Pamphilius, was unable to explain original chaos[4]—the state of the universe before a divine creator supposedly separated heaven and earth.[5]

Yearning for a more scientific understanding of the world's origins, the young Epicurus abandoned the religion-oriented teachings of Plato in favour of the physics-oriented teachings of Democritus—the esteemed 'father of modern science'.[6] Such a prestigious title came from Democritus' ground-breaking (and evidently accurate) theory that everything in the universe is composed of microscopic bodies called atoms.[7]

Epicurus largely agreed with this concept, but doubted Democritus' explanation of how such atoms move; rather than accept their rigid, non-interactive and pre-determined motion downward, Epicurus suggested that *some* atoms might occasionally 'swerve' to the side and collide with one another.[8] These random, microscopic collisions, he argued, eventually accumulate to form macroscopic bodies, for if this were not the case, it is feasible that the universe—the ultimate macroscopic body—would have never been created.[9]

Beyond scientifically explaining the universe's origins, Epicurus' theory of the atomic swerve would have broad implications for philosophy, particularly on Epicurus' understanding of how humans ought to live; he reasoned that if *atoms* are not set on a pre-determined path, then *humans* are similarly unchained by determinism.[10] Therefore, just as atoms are not inherently restricted to move in a certain way, people, Epicurus argued, should exercise this same metaphorical freedom 'to swerve' by living as they please.

---

3   Hiram Crispo, *Tending the Epicurean Garden* (Washington D.C: American Humanist Association, 2014), 9.
4   Crispo, *Tending the Epicurean Garden*, 10.
5   Douglas Harper, 'Chaos', *Online Etymology Dictionary,* accessed on 20 April 2016, http://www.dictionary.com/browse/chaos.
6   Sharon David Rives, *Epicurus and the Modern Mind* (Washington D.C: The World and I Online, 2014), 4–6.
7   Rives, *Epicurus and the Modern Mind*, 4–6.
8   Stephen Greenblatt, *The Swerve: How the World Became Modern* (New York, NY: W.W. Norton & Company, 2011), 3.
9   Tim O'Keefe, 'Epicurus (341-271 B.C.E)', *Internet Encyclopedia of Philosophy,* accessed on 20 April 2016, http://www.iep.utm.edu/epicur/#SSH3c.ii.
10 Rives, *Epicurus and the Modern Mind*, 8–12.

2 Epicurus' Conception of Happiness

This now-famous philosophy, in which pleasure is life's chief good and ultimate pursuit, is formally defined as 'hedonism'.[11] Epicurus adopted this notion, writing:

> we must exercise ourselves in the things which bring happiness, since, if that be present, we have everything, and, if that be absent, all our actions are directed towards attaining it.[12]

But what are these 'things which bring happiness'? Before recognizing the explicit pursuits that *do* bring happiness, Epicurus notoriously suggested two domains that do *not*: politics and religion.

Such overt hostility towards politics might be partially explained by the corrupt political climate of 3rd century B.C Athens—a time of crumbled empires, tyrannical rulers, and general government mistrust.[13] Yet Epicurus' stance seems primarily justified by his conviction that our limited time on earth should be spent pursuing more pleasure-oriented endeavours, for Epicurus argued there is no form of natural happiness *the state* exclusively delivers.[14] As such, in opposition to Plato and Aristotle—both of who encouraged an active interest in justice[15]—, Epicurus recommended man abstain from political affairs entirely.[16]

Yet more than politics, Epicurus noted how *religion* would often detract from man's pursuit of pleasure; he observed how both the fear of death and hope for a pleasurable afterlife tended to severely restrict how people would live in their earthly lives. But by denouncing the potential of the soul's immortality, reasoning that human existence—encompassing both body and soul—terminates entirely upon death, Epicurus invalidated these fears and hopes: 'Death is

---

11 'Hedonism', *Dictionary.com Unabridged*, accessed on 20 April 2016, http://www.dictionary.com/browse/hedonism.
12 Vincent Cook, 'Epicurus & Epicurean Philosophy', *Epicurus.net*, accessed on 20 April 2016, http://www.epicurus.net/en/menoeceus.html.
13 Rives, *Epicurus and the Modern Mind*, 2.
14 Crispo, *Tending the Epicurean Garden*, 16.
15 Justin Wendling, 'Aristotle and Epicurus', *Rebirth of Reason TM*, accessed on 20 April 2016, http://rebirthofreason.com/Articles/Wendling/Aristotle_and_Epicurus.shtml.
16 The Stanford Encyclopedia of Philosophy, 'Epicurus', *Stanford University*, accessed on 20 April 2016, http://plato.stanford.edu/entries/epicurus/.

nothing to us; for that which has been dissolved into its elements experiences no sensations, and that which has no sensation is nothing to us'.[17]

Therefore, Epicurus deduced, if we are *unconscious* for death, then it is fruitless to spend our *conscious* lives fearing it, especially if this fear limits our pursuit of pleasure. After all, just as he observed of those who try to appease the state to avoid political and economic misfortune, trying to appease the gods to avoid a miserable afterlife would often produce more disappointment than gratification.

This formulaic reasoning, expressed as the idea that the pain of actions should never exceed their pleasure, was called *aponia*.[18] Literally translated as the 'removal of all pain', *aponia* marked one of three key tenets of Epicurean happiness. As Epicurus explained:

> The magnitude of pleasure reaches its limit in the removal of all pain. When the pleasure is present, so long as it is uninterrupted, there is no pain either of body or of mind or both together.[19]

Under *aponia*, we may understand, for instance, how eating is only 'pleasurable' to the extent it does not cause short-term pain, such as a stomach-ache, or long-term pain, such as diabetes (e.g the difference between one piece of chocolate and one hundred pieces of chocolate.)

But far more than physical pain, Epicurus despised the *emotional* pain of anxiety, and thus contended we practice *ataraxia*, 'peace and freedom from fear'.[20] Through this second condition, he meant that we, consistent with the randomly swerving atoms that comprise us, should not stick to the conventions of any pre-determined path, like politics or religion or material success. Instead, Epicurus proposed our happiness is best insured and fear best minimized if we provide for it ourselves:

> Being godlike—that is, self-sufficient, without care, confusion, and dependency on others—is the prescription for our happiness. The gods have naught to do with humankind, but our happiness depends upon our imitation of them.[21]

---

17 Cook, 'Epicurus & Epicurean Philosophy'.
18 Crispo, *Tending the Epicurean Garden*, 60.
19 Cook, 'Epicurus & Epicurean Philosophy'.
20 Crispo, *Tending the Epicurean Garden*, 10.
21 Cook, 'Epicurus & Epicurean Philosophy'.

This credo of 'self-sufficiency' was aptly practiced at Epicurus' school. Appropriately named Ho Kepos (The Garden), the Epicurean academy, unlike that of Plato or Aristotle, was constructed upon a private lawn, outside of Athens' city centre, behind the tiny abode he shared with many friends.[22] Guided by its founder's vehement belief in human freedom and rejection of deterministic conventions, Epicurus' school admitted both women and slaves as students, an allowance unheard of in 3rd century B.C.[23]

Yet perhaps the most shocking characteristic of Ho Kepos was the extreme moderation followers practiced in their eating and drinking habits. Contrary to his legacy of luxury, Epicurus' daily diet consisted merely of water and barley cakes; only on a special occasion would the philosopher treat himself and his students to indulge in 'gourmet' items like wine and cheese.[24] Not only did this intense rationing allegedly enable Ho Kepos to survive one of Athens' most devastating famines, but consuming in moderation, like avoiding politics and religion, further empowered the Epicureans to focus on more meaningful pursuits.

The nature of these pursuits was elucidated through Epicurus' third condition of pleasure—the avoidance of *kenodoxia*, 'empty and unnecessary beliefs and desires' for things like money, power and sex, in lieu of *natural* desires, like wisdom.[25] Such a theory is highlighted in Epicurus' Letter to Menoeceus:

> Let no one be slow to seek wisdom. ... no age is too early or too late for the health of the soul. And to say that the season for studying philosophy has not yet come ... is like saying that the season for happiness is not yet or that it is now no more.[26]

This idea of happiness as 'health for the soul' makes great sense in the context of Epicurus' theory of a non-deterministic universe. For instance, because purely physical pleasures, such as eating a cheeseburger, produce uniform, purely physical effects amongst those who experience them, Epicurus would call these pleasures 'unnecessary', insofar as they neither require nor benefit from the exercise of free will; there seems to be nothing epistemologically unique about eating a cheeseburger.

---

22 Crispo, *Tending the Epicurean Garden*, 12.
23 Ibid, 16.
24 Ibid, 12.
25 The Stanford Encyclopedia of Philosophy, 'Epicurus'.
26 Epicurus, 'Letter to Menoeceus', trans. Vincent Cook, *Epicurus.net*, accessed 20 April 2016, http://www.epicurus.net/en/menoeceus.html.

But pleasures of the mind, such as a philosophical conversation, *are* largely individualized; they *do not* produce a uniform result amongst those who experience them, and thus *do* depend on free will. Given this theory, Epicurus believed the active and collaborative contemplation of how we can best live on earth constitutes life's 'fullest' desire; no 'empty', physical sensation could supersede such a natural pleasure, an idea which a dying Epicurus reiterated in his Letter to Idomeneus:

> I have been attacked by a painful inability to urinate, and also dysentery, so violent that nothing can be added to the violence of my sufferings. But the cheerfulness of my mind, which comes from the recollection of all my philosophical contemplation, counterbalances all these afflictions.[27]

3   History's Distortion of Epicurean Happiness

Having established *aponia* and *ataraxia,* as well as avoiding *kenodoxia,* to be necessary conditions of Epicurus' happiness, we can more clearly understand the drastic extent to which 'epicurean' happiness as a *physical* sensation has been distorted. We know this distortion occurred somewhere in between 270 B.C—the year of his death—, and the 19th century—the era in which 'epicurean' was first recorded to mean 'luxurious' or 'gourmet'—,[28] yet the mystery of how Epicurus' ideas about happiness became so inaccurately interpreted remains. However, because we also know that true epicurean pleasure necessarily entailed freedom from religion and politics—two immensely important and controversial institutions in Common Era history—, we should begin by examining how such institutions perceived Epicurus.

In the Rabbinical Talmudic *Mishnah,* for example, Epicurus is denounced for his agnostic beliefs. Written in the second century A.D, the ancient text asserts 'Epicureans. ... do not merit the world come'.[29] This agnostic association carried into modern Judaism, under which the generic term 'apikoros [Epicurus]' refers to a non-believer.[30]

But early Christianity went a step further by simultaneously criticizing Epicurus' agnosticism and hedonism. Because early Christians, like the early Jews,

---

27   Epicurus, 'Letter to Idiomeneus', trans. Vincent Cook, *Epicurus.net*, accessed 20 April 2016, http://www.epicurus.net/en/idomeneus.html.
28   'Epicurean', *Dictionary.com*.
29   Cook, 'Epicurus & Epicurean Philosophy'.
30   Cook, 'Epicurus & Epicurean Philosophy'.

understandably opposed agnosticism, they were highly unlikely to give consideration to the nuances of epicurean pleasure. For instance, as Ambrose of Milan's wrote in 396 A.D to the Christian congregation at Vercellae:

> Epicurus himself ... whom these persons think they should follow rather than the apostles ... denies that pleasure brings in evil, does not deny that certain things result from it from which evils are generated; and asserts in fine that the life of the luxurious which is filled with pleasures does not seem to be reprehensible.[31]

Angered by the prospect of people 'follow[ing Epicurus] rather than the apostles' and thus pursuing happiness over piety, Ambrose reduced Epicurus' concept of pleasure to a 'life of luxur[y]' as opposed to a life of active contemplation. Such a distortion seems intentional, for it was probably far easier for the early Christians to vilify a life 'filled with [*physical*] pleasures' as sinful and evil than it was to vilify *mental* pleasures like freedom and truth. For the next 1400 years, this Christian hostility remained, as Epicurean teachings were often banned and texts often burned.[32] As summarized by historian Vincent Cook, 'the Christian faith had emerged victorious over the cause of human happiness and rationality'.[33]

Yet when the Enlightenment swept Europe in the 18th century, the influence of religion on rationality decreased considerably. As such, when French philosopher Pierre Gassendi revived Epicureanism in the mid-17th century, his focus was not on Epicurus' agnosticism, but rather on his theory of atomism.[34] This was iterated in Roman poet Lucretius (99–55 B.C)' recently discovered *De Rurum Natura*, in which he references Epicurus' theory to conclude that the randomness of atomic motion is needed to 'break the bonds of [human] fate'.[35]

Such revolutionary ideas about the cosmos profoundly influenced Enlightenment thinkers before eventually reaching American founding father Thomas Jefferson. Yet when this self-proclaimed Epicurean paradoxically enshrined 'the pursuit of happiness' in the Declaration of Independence, he

---

31   St. Ambrose, 'Letter 63', trans. Kevin Knight, *New Advent,* accessed 20 April 2016, http://www.newadvent.org/fathers/340963.htm.
32   Alexander of Abonoteichus, 'Letter to Celsus', trans. A. M. Harmon, *Loeb Classical Library,* accessed 20 April 2016, http://www.tertullian.org/rpearse/lucian/lucian_alexander.htm.
33   Cook, 'Epicurus & Epicurean Philosophy'.
34   Ibid.
35   Greenblatt, *The Swerve: How the World Became Modern*, 3.

had inadvertently contradicted Epicurus' recommendation to avoid political affairs.[36] Furthermore, by failing to specify the *nature* of happiness Americans should pursue, Jefferson, much like the early Christians, had *reduced* Epicurean happiness to 'sensual pleasure', and promoted misguided notions like the American Dream.

This misconstrued notion of 'epicurean' pleasure as a physical sensation carried into the 19th and 20th centuries, during which the term became increasingly popular. For instance, in an excerpt from a 1931 issue of *Astounding Stories*, the phrase 'epicurean meal' was used to describe a luxurious, gourmet dinner.[37] Earlier, in an 1869 edition of *Nautical Magazine*, 'epicurean' was similarly employed to connote extreme pleasure: 'Southern races are sometimes indolent, but rarely Epicurean in their habits; it is the Northern man who sighs for his fleshpots'.[38]

In analysing such an excerpt, we note how associating Epicurean habits with the pursuit of 'flesh-pots', defined as 'sensual pleasure' or 'sexual gratification', further deviates from the core values of Epicurus, who denounced sex under the condition of *kenodoxia*.

But we may also note how the author *associated* Epicurean habits with the urban-dwelling Northerner and *contrasted* them with the 'indolent', farm-dwelling Southerner. Because this excerpt was written during the Industrial Revolution, an era which eroded the self-sufficiency of the South and idolized the industrialized 'efficiency' of the North, the association seems inaccurate in terms of true 'epicurean' values. Indeed, when considering Epicurus' simultaneous praise for modest, contemplative living and disdain for material, unnecessary desires, it seems Epicurus would have much preferred the 'indolent' yet self-sufficient Southerner over the pleasure-seeking, yet misguided Northerner.

4 The Return of True Epicurean Happiness

Author Tim Kreider boldly defended such 'indolence' in 'The Busy Trap', a viral *New York Times* editorial published in 2012. Inviting readers to question the purpose of the 'busy-ness' to which they've obligated themselves, Kreider explains how most of our schedule packing is a response to the

---

36 Crispo, *Tending the Epicurean Garden*, 16.
37 Arthur Leo Zagat and Nat Schacner, 'The Death Cloud', *Astounding Stories,* May 1931.
38 *The Nautical Magazine and Naval Chronicle for 1869,* New York: Cambridge University Press, 2013.

'fear of what [people] might have to face in its absence'.[39] But like Epicurus, Kreider believes that the end—money, luxury, power, material success—to which we often attribute our busyness is not something that will actually bring us happiness. Instead, as Kreider mentions in his conclusion, 'the best investment of [our] limited time on earth is to spend it with the people [we] love'.[40]

In reiterating Epicurus' theory of pleasure, insofar as it condemns the empty pursuit of material wealth and encourages the active pursuit of philosophy with friends, Kreider awakes an existential nerve in his readers, as he understands how the legitimacy of the American dream—the promise which suggests hard work will yield material wealth, and material wealth will yield happiness—is fading. Upon surveying 450,000 U.S residents, in 2010, to determine the age old question if money buys happiness, Daniel Kahneman of Princeton University found that 'high income does *not* improve emotional well-being'.[41] The 10,000 Millennials recently polled by Viacom's Scratch echoed these results, with 64% claiming they would 'rather make $40,000 a year at a job they love than $100,000 a year at a job they think is boring'.[42]

But beyond statistics, we see the erosion of the "bigger is better" credo prevalent in formal efforts, such as the Tiny House movement. Based on 'environmental concerns, financial concerns, and the desire for more time and freedom', the Tiny House movement mobilizes people to '*choose* to downsize the space they live in'.[43] In an era where most Americans devote 33 to 50% of their income to their home,[44] the movement strives to reverse such financial trends, while simultaneously reversing the classic American 'bigger-is-better' credo.

A similar ethos is prevalent within the Slow Food movement, which aims to preserve local food cultures and utilize agriculture of the local ecosystem.[45] Founded

---

39   Tim Kreider, 'The Busy Trap', *New York Times,* accessed 20 April 2016, http://opinionator.blogs.nytimes.com/2012/06/30/the-busy-trap/?_r=0.

40   Kreider, 'The Busy Trap'.

41   Daniel Kahneman and Angus Deaton, 'High Income Improves Evaluation of Life but Not Emotional Well-Being'. *Proceedings of the National Academy of Sciences* 107 (38): 16489–16493.

42   Scratch/Viacom Media Networks, *The Millennial Disruption Index,* accessed 20 April 2016, http://www.millennialdisruptionindex.com.

43   Ryan Mitchell, 'What Is the Tiny House Movement', *The Tiny Life,* 12 May 2010.

44   Mary Schwartz, and Ellen Wilson, 'Who Can Afford to Live in a Home?: A Look at Data from the 2006 American Community Survey', *US Census Bureau,* accessed 20 April 2016, https://www.census.gov/housing/census/publications/who-can-afford.pdf.

45   Carlo Petrini, *Slow Food: The Case for Taste* (New York: Columbia University Press, 2003).

in 1989 to oppose the construction of a McDonald's, the Slow Food movement attempts to bring consumers closer to the food they eat by encouraging localized 'self-sufficiency' over globalization. Other increasingly popular eating trends, such as the Whole30 movement and the Paleolithic lifestyle ('Paleo') movement, bear a similar goal; by promoting natural foods and opposing processed foods, these movements collectively echo both Epicurus' theory of self-sufficiency and practice of 'eating to live', rather than living to eat.[46]

While each of these aforementioned movements channels a specific element of Epicurus' philosophy, efforts such as 'International Downshifting Week' and the 'Simplicity Collective' reflect Epicurus' broader conceptions of happiness. Defined as a campaign to promote the simple life, both initiatives recommend tangible tips—like cooking a meal from scratch, cutting up a credit card, and handcrafting a letter—on how to practice such downshifting[47] and voluntary simplicity.[48]

Though yet to be labelled 'epicurean', these economic, environmental and cultural movements signify how Epicurus' *true* conceptions of happiness are finally re-emerging after a 2400-year history of distortion. And while we have a long way to go before epicurean simplicity is fully re-embraced, we are beginning to understand, as Epicurus would say, how 'he who is not satisfied with a little, is satisfied with nothing'.

Bibliography

Alexander of Abonoteichus. 'Letter to Celsus'. Translated by A. M. Harmon Harvard: Loeb Classical Library, 1936.

Crispo, Hiram. *Tending the Epicurean Garden*. Washington D.C: American Humanist Association, 2014. Kindle.

Cook, Vincent. 'Epicurus & Epicurean Philosophy'. *Epicurus.net,* 4 December 1996. Accessed 20 April 2016. http://www.epicurus.net/.

'Epicurean'. *Dictionary.com*. Accessed 20 April 2016. http://www.dictionary.com/browse.epicurean.

---

46 Samantha Chang, 'Whole30 Diet, a Hardcore Version of Paleo Diet, Promises Quick Weight Loss', *The Examiner,* accessed 20 April 2016, http://www.examiner.com/article/extreme-version-of-paleo-diet-rises-popularity.

47 Tracey West, 'International Downshifting Week', *Swan Developments,* accessed 20 April 2016, http://www.downshiftingweek.com/.

48 Cook, 'Epicurus & Epicurean Philosophy'.

'Epicurus'. *The Stanford Encyclopedia of Philosophy*. Stanford University, 2014. Accessed 20 April 2016. http://plato.stanford.edu/entries/epicurus/.

Epicurus. 'Letter to Menoeceus'. *Epicurus & Epicurean Philosophy*. Translated by Vincent Cook. 1996. Accessed 20 April 2016. http://www.epicurus.net/en/menoeceus.html.

Epicurus. 'Letter to Idomeneus'. *Epicurus & Epicurean Philosophy*. Translated by Vincent Cook. 1996. Accessed 20 April 2016. http://www.epicurus.net/en/idomeneus.html.

Greenblatt, Stephen. *The Swerve: How the World Became Modern.* New York: W.W. Norton & Company, 2011.

Harper, Douglas. s.v. 'Chaos'. *Dictionary.com*. Accessed 20 April 2016. http://www.dictionary.com/browse/chaos.

'Hedonism'. *Dictionary.com*. Accessed 20 April 2016. http://www.dictionary.com/browse/hedonism.

Lucretius. *De Rurum Natura,* Translated by Stephen Greenblatt. New York: W.W. Norton & Company, 2011.

Kahneman, Daniel and Angus Deaton. 'High Income Improves Evaluation of Life but Not Emotional Well-Being'. *Proceedings of the National Academy of Sciences* 107.38 (2013): 16489–16493.

Kreider, Tim. 'The Busy Trap'. *The New York Times*, 30 June 2012. Accessed 20 April 2016. http://opinionator.blogs.nytimes.com/2012/06/30/the-busy-trap/?_r=0.

Mitchell, Ryan. 'What Is the Tiny House Movement'. *The Tiny Life,* 12 May 2010.

The Nautical Magazine and Naval Chronicle for 1869. New York: Cambridge University Press, 2013.

O'Keefe, Tim. 'Epicurus (341-271 B.C.E)'. *Internet Encyclopedia of Philosophy,* 1995. Accessed 20 April 2016. http://www.iep.utm.edu/epicur/#SSH3c.ii.

Rives, Sharon David. *Epicurus and the Modern Mind.* Washington D.C: The World and I Online, 2014. Kindle.

Scratch/Viacom Media Networks. *The Millennial Disruption Index.* 2014. Accessed 20 April 2016. http://www.millennialdisruptionindex.com/.

St. Ambrose. 'Letter 63'. Translated by Kevin Knight. Buffalo, NY: New Advent, 2009. Accessed 20 April 2016. http://www.newadvent.org/fathers/34o963.htm.

Thompson, Derek. 'America's Weird, Enduring Love Affair with Cars and Houses'. *The Atlantic,* 25 February 2014.

Wendling, Justin. 'Aristotle and Epicurus'. *Rebirth of Reason TM.* 1 December 2005. Accessed 20 April 2016. http://rebirthofreason.com/Articles/Wendling/Aristotle_and_Epicurus.shtml.

West, Tracey. 'International Downshifting Week', *Swan Developments,* 2003. Accessed 20 April 2016. http://www.downshiftingweek.com/.

Zagat, Arthur Leo and Nat Schacner. 'The Death Cloud'. *Astounding Stories,* May 1931.

CHAPTER 15

The Subjective Well-Being of Married Women In and Out of the Workforce in Sri Lanka

Ann Shelomi Panditharatne

Abstract

This study investigates the socio-economic factors that are associated with subjective well-being of married Sri Lankan women by considering their life satisfaction levels and to find out whether going out to work, in addition to their other care-giving responsibilities, makes married working women's subjective well-being higher than those who do not engage in market work. Female labour force participation in Sri Lanka is one of the lowest in the world and is half of the male participation rate. Married women report the lowest labour force participation. Role theory is used to identify the impact on a woman's subjective well-being when assuming multiple roles, especially with regards to playing the role of an employee in addition to other care giving roles she plays. The conceptual framework includes all roles which a married woman plays throughout her life such as daughter, wife, mother, daughter-in-law, and employee. Data was collected through a cross sectional household survey. The representative sample consists of 838 respondents from 845 households. Study finds that going out to work, in addition to their other care-giving responsibilities, makes married working women's subjective well-being lower than homemakers. We also find that being happily married, well appreciated, having children who are doing well in life, being able to achieve childhood goals, and being able to easily manage monthly expenses, all seems to be having a positive impact on married women's happiness. However, women who feel that they are burdened with household duties, and women who consider their own living standards to be much lower than the reference category, seem to be relatively unhappy.

Keywords

subjective well-being – roles – women – work

1 Introduction

It can be argued that all developmental activities, aim to increase people's overall well–being. Therefore, identifying the correlates of well-being, both objective well-being and subjective well-being has important policy implications.[1] The available evidence from the Annual World Happiness Survey suggests that Sri Lanka is one of the few countries in which one out of every five people has stated that they are *suffering* in life.[2] This seems to imply that the development process has not delivered acceptable levels of well-being to at least a fifth of the country's population.

However, to date there have been only a limited number of studies of subjective well-being in Sri Lanka.[3] The subjective well-being of Sri Lankans in and out of the labour force has not received any attention at all, even though there is growing international literature that focuses on subjective well-being related to labour market outcomes. The issue of the subjective well-being of working women, in particular, has drawn the attention of scholars working in this area. The international empirical evidence suggests that employment has positive effects on a woman either as a primary source of well-being (gained through external social networks at work, financial security and sense of identity) or as a buffer against the strain associated with other roles that she needs to play.[4] However, other studies suggest that continuously drawing from emotional resources and limited time to balance multiple roles of worker, mother, wife, and daughter as women almost invariably do, can reduce a woman's subjective well-being.[5]

None of the Sri Lankan studies on subjective well-being cited above has looked at the specific issue of how employment affects married women's

---

1 Courtland Smith and Patricia Clay, 'Measuring Subjective and Objective Well-Being: Analyses from Five Marine Commercial Fisheries', *Human Organization* 69.2 (2010): 158–168; objective well-being – independently observable assessment of conditions; subjective well-being subjective measures by which people measure their own lives.
2 Bryant Ott, *More Sri Lankans Suffering since the War Ended*, viewed 16 February 2013, http://www.gallup.com/poll/153779/Sri-Lankans-Suffering-War-Ended.aspx
3 Chaminda Weerackody and Saman Fernando, *Reflections on Mental Health and Well-Being, Learning from Communities Affected by Conflict, Dislocation and Natural Disasters in Sri Lanka*, (Colombo: People's Rural Development Association (PRADA),2011); Sanjeewanie Kariyawasam,Nilakshi De Silva and Shivapragasam Shivakumaran, 'Multi-Dimensional Poverty among Samurdhi Welfare Recipients in Badulla District Sri Lanka', *PMMA Working Paper*,2012-03 (2012):Partnership for Economic Policy, Centre for Poverty Analysis, Sri Lanka.
4 Rosalind Barnett and Grace K. Baruch, 'Women's Involvement in Multiple Roles, Role Strain, and Psychological Distress',*Journal of Personality and Social Psychology* 49(1985): 135–145.
5 Arlie R. Hochschild, *The Time Bind: When Work Becomes Home and Home Becomes Work* (New York: Henry Holy,1997).

subjective well-being. However, this is an important issue because it has been officially recognized that Sri Lanka's national employment strategy needs to identify and address the major barriers that women face in the labour market because the country's future growth prospects are dependent on more women engaging in market work.[6] Sri Lanka has the twentieth (out of 163 countries) largest gap in labour force participation between the sexes in the world.[7] As a result of the free education and health system, Sri Lankan women are well placed in terms of education, health and family systems compared to their counterparts in South Asia.[8] However women's educational gains have not translated into substantial increases in their labour force participation. Married women have the lowest rates of labour force participation and majority of married Sri Lankan women are unable to participate in the labour force due to domestic work and childcare activities.[9] However, it should also be noted that women who are in the labour force contribute significantly to the national income as they engage in the key foreign exchange earning sectors, such as export-oriented agriculture, manufacturing and overseas employment.[10]

This paper attempts to find whether going out to work, in addition to their other care-giving responsibilities, makes married working women's subjective well-being higher than those who do not engage in market work through the means of a quantitative economic analysis of subjective well-being.

2   Literature Survey

Several empirical studies in the international literature examine the psychological effects of work on women, mainly focusing on broad comparisons between

---

6   Ministry of Labour Relations and Manpower, Central Bank of Sri Lanka, Department of Census and Statistics, 'Labour and Social Trends in Sri Lanka', *Recent Economic Labour Market and Social Developments* (2009): 6.
7   Ministry of Labour Relations and Manpower, 'Labour and Social Trends'; United Nations Development Programme (UNDP) Sri Lanka, *Sri Lanka Human Development Report 2012: Bridging Regional Disparities for Human Development* (Colombo:UNDP Sri Lanka, 2012).
8   Ramani Gunatilaka, 'Women's Participation in Sri Lanka's Labour Force: Trends, Drivers and Constraints', *ILO Asia-Pacific Working Paper Series*, (2013): ILO Sub Regional Office for South Asia, New Delhi.
9   Amara J. Satharasinghe, 'Time-Use Analysis of Husbands and Wives', *Sri Lanka Journal of Population Studies* 2 (1999): 11–24; Gunatilaka, 'Women's Participation', 10.
10 International Labour Organization (ILO), 'Globalization, Employment and Gender in the Open Economy of Sri Lanka', *Employment Working Paper Series*, 138 (2013): Employment Sector, Employment Policy Department.

homemakers and employed women.[11] Mary Clare Lennon, a sociologist in United States compared employed wives and full-time homemakers based on characteristics of their daily work activities and the consequences of these work conditions for psychological well-being.[12] She found that as a result of the different configurations of their work characteristics, employed wives and homemakers experience on average similar levels of lower well-being.[13] This finding is supported by a recent cross country research carried out using 20,588 observations in 57 countries by Beja, Jr. who found no clear difference in the happiness between the working wife and the housewife.[14] Beja.J further suggests that in all cases where there is a disparity between the subjective well-being of the housewife and the working wife, it is not generally due to individual characteristics and the attitude of the wife, but due to the culture and the social context.

It's also found that women's labour force participation decisions and subjective well-being are significantly associated with the gender inequalities in the distribution of domestic duties.[15] The study by Alvarez and Miles used 23,995 observations from the Survey of the Quality of Work from Spain and used identity-ideology models to examine the relationship between domestic duties and subjective well-being which they found to be clearly negative.[16]

On the other hand, available data on well-being in Sri Lanka, suggests that an employed wife on average spends 4.8 hours on house work, 3.2 hours on childcare 7.9 hours on family work and 8.0 on paid work; which comes to a staggering 15.9 hours per day whereas the husband's total work time (paid work as well as housework) comes to 13.8 hours.[17] The study indicates that 'gender is the strongest determinant of total housework time. Employed women spend longer than their husbands on housework, whatever their paid work time, or sex role ideologies are'.[18]

---

11 Mary C. Lennon, 'Women, Work and Well-Being: The Importance of Work Conditions', *Journal of Health and Social Behaviour* 35 (1994): 235–247; Katarina Boye, 'Work and Well-Being in a Comparative Perspective – The Role of Family Policy', *European Sociological Review* 27.1 (2011): 16–30.
12 Lennon, 'Women, Work and Well-Being'.
13 Lennon, 'Women, Work and Well-Being'.
14 Edsel L. Beja Jr, 'Who is Happier: House Wife or Working Wife?', *Applied Research in Quality of Life*, 9 (2014): 157–177.
15 Begona Alvarez and Daniel Miles, *Women's Subjective Well-Being and Housework Allocation*, (Spain: Department of Applied Economics, University of Vigo, 2012).
16 Alvarez and Miles, 'Women's Subjective Well-Being'.
17 Satharasinghe, 'Time-Use Analysis of Husbands and Wives'.
18 Satharasinghe, 'Time-Use Analysis of Husbands and Wives', 20.

The decisions of women and mothers, for or against employment are not merely based on rational cost-benefit calculations, but are also influenced by cultural factors to a significant extent. Using data from seven European countries, Henning et al., a group of German sociologists, found that culturally shaped role images can result in mothers being pictured as being solely responsible for the care and upbringing of children.[19] These findings are further supported by Malhotra and DeGraff's study on Sri Lankan women, which found that, 'Employment status of women maybe a reflection not only of economic need, individual ability, and individual preferences but also of culturally appropriate definitions of women's roles according to marital status'.[20] Sanjeewanie's study further found that given the nature of the cultural context in which they live, men always expected the women to be full time homemakers and take care of children, though women are in most cases more educated than males. The following statement by a 52 year old female respondent, explains this point further,

> My husband doesn't want me to do a job, because he wants me to stay at home and look after our children, *not only that his parents also*. But I did a job before the marriage, at that time, I had enough money in my hand to use as my own, but now I have to depend on my husband. If I could do a job I can help him to share the household expenses. But he says he can do that.[21]

3 Theory

In general a married woman's life tends to be structured by the experiences and the expectations of husbands, children, aging parents/in laws; and these relationships are formed through sets of roles. This is why it's important to look at the different roles married women play throughout their lives when discussing their subjective well-being. In this context, role theory is ideal as it's

---

19   Marina Hennig et al., 'How do Employed Women Perceive the Reconciliation of Work and Family Life?: A Seven-Country Comparison of The Impact of Family Policies on Women's Employment', *International Journal of Sociology and Social Policy*, 32.9 (2012): 513–529.

20   Anju Malhotra, and Deborah S. Degraff, 'Daughters and Wives: Marital Status, Poverty and Young Women's Employment in Sri Lanka', *Women Poverty and Demographic Change*, ed. Brigida Garcia (Oxford: Oxford University Press Inc, 2000), 146.

21   Sanjeewanie Kariyawasam 2012, 'Comparative Perspective: Gendered Dimensions of Well-Being' (Paper Presented at the 13th National convention on Women's Studies, Centre for Women's Research Sri Lanka, July 27–30, 2012): 10.

based on two contradictory processes: role strain and role enhancement. Role strain argues that assuming multiple roles is detrimental to well-being.[22] Role enhancement argues that engaging in multiple roles enhances well-being.[23] Role theory assumes that there is no reverse causality between roles and subjective well-being.

4 Methodology

Due to unavailability of secondary data, primary data was collected through a household survey. Purposive sampling was used to select the Province, District and the Divisional Secretariat in which the household survey was carried. Considering logistical and costs factors, employment opportunities and infrastructure facilities, Western Province was selected. Within Western Province Kalutara district was selected mainly because it had the highest female labour force participation rates and highest percentage in economically inactive population due to housework, which is ideal for this research.[24] Pandura Divisional Secretariat was selected as its population dense compared to other Divisional Secretaries within Kalutara district.[25] Fifteen GN Divisions in Panadura were identified as suitable for data collection based on the ethno religion mix of the population and the number of employed women.[26] The sample comprised of 838 respondents from 845 households. The following happiness function was used to model the subjective well-being of individuals.

$$W_{it} = \alpha + \beta X_{it} + \varepsilon_{it}$$

---

22 William J. Goode, 'A Theory of Strain', *American Sociological Review* 25 (1960): 483–496; Role strain theory is also known as scarcity hypothesis.

23 Stephen R. Marks, 'Multiple Roles and Role Strain: Some Notes on Human Energy, Time and Commitment', *American Sociological Review,* 41 (1977): 921–936; Role enhancement theory is also known as expansion hypothesis.

24 Department of Census and Statistics, *Census of Population and Housing 2012* (Colombo: Ministry of Finance and Planning, 2012); Department of Census and Statistics, *Sri Lanka Labour Force Survey Annual Report 2012* (Colombo: Ministry of Finance and Planning, 2012).

25 Department of Census and Statistics, Census of Population.

26 GN Division – Grama Niladhari Division is a sub unit of the Divisional Secretariat can be considered as the first level administrative unit.

In the equation above, the dependent variable, W_{it} is some self-reported level of happiness of individual i at time t. The respondent was asked, overall, how do you feel about life these days?, to which she selected an integer on the life satisfaction scale that extends from 1 to 6, where 1 denotes *not happy at all*, 2 denotes *not happy*, 3 denotes *just so so*, 4 denotes *happy*, 5 denotes *very happy* and 6 denotes *Don't know/can't say*. The term α is the constant and β is the coefficient of vector X containing socio-demographic and socioeconomic characteristics, or environmental, social, institutional, and economic conditions for individual i at time t. ε_{it} is the error term which captures the individual differences in reporting and the impact of variables that are correlated with happiness but are not included in the model. This study will estimate OLS estimates of the happiness score, both with a basic specification and with a full set of explanatory variables.[27]

All variables which seemed probable of influencing happiness were included. Dummy variables were used as devices to sort data into mutually exclusive categories when handling nominal-categorical explanatory variables. In addition, explanatory variables with cardinal values were assigned to qualitative assessments so that greater intensity is represented by a higher value.

According to Sociology literature, most important factors a women considers when reconciling work and family life are the household work load, family policy and the presence of children in the household.[28] Household work was represented by two variables, *the number of hours spent doing housework per day* and the respondent's explanation as to why she engaged in housework as in the dummy variable there is *no one else to do housework*. This variable took the value one if the respondent did most of the housework by herself as there was no one else to do it, as opposed to the situation where other family members did help out with housework. The variable extent to which she is being appreciated by family, denoted the responses received to the question, '*Generally, when you think of yourself and what you do looking after everybody, how do you feel?*', to which five possible answers ranging from 'very much appreciated' to 'not at all appreciated', were converted into a cardinal variable whose value increased with the extent to which the respondent felt that she was appreciated by family. The relational concerns of subjective well-being are involved in comparing the shared notions of the good life. In this view, subjective well-being is the gap between perceptions of life-as-it-is with notions of

---

27   OLS – ordinary least squares.
28   Hennig, et al., 'How do employed women perceive'; family policy – (time and domestic duty segregation among the family members).

how-life-should-be[29]. Taking this into consideration respondents were asked about their childhood goals (i.e. whether they wanted to be a career woman, a homemaker or both) and their perceptions of goal achievement (i.e. fulfilled/ not fulfilled) were recorded.

It's found that a woman's satisfaction with life is mainly based on her relationships, connections and networks.[30] Thus respondents were asked about how they perceive their relationships with husbands/parents/in laws. When asked to describe each of these relationships, respondent selected an integer on the scale that extends from 1 to 6, where 1 denotes *distant*, 2 denotes *not close*, 3 denotes *just so so*, 4 denotes *close*, 5 denotes *very close* and 6 denotes *Don't know/can't say*. Previous research has shown that women's perceptions about children play a major role in determining their subjective well-being associated with motherhood.[31] Accordingly, respondents were asked how they perceive the well-being of their children; to which they could select from *doing very well, doing well, just so so, disappointing,* and *very disappointing*.

Income is one of the most commonly researched areas in happiness studies. It is found that income increases happiness, ceteris paribus, but only up to a point where basic needs are fulfilled. Beyond that, happiness is dependent on individual aspiration levels which are influenced by the process of adaption and social comparison.[32] Hence in addition to absolute income related variables such as household income, expenditure, opinion on monthly income/ expenditure; we also included variables on relative income as economic variables. For this we included some proxies for income comparisons such as comparison of current living standards to past living standards and information about their reference groups; as its found that people's aspirations are influenced by their reference groups.[33]

---

[29] Alex C. Michalos, 'Multiple discrepancies theory (MDT)', *Social indicators research* 16. 4 (1985): 347–413.

[30] Wendy Campione, W, James Morgan, and Max Jerrell, 'Employed Women's Wellbeing: The Global and Daily Impact of Work', Working Paper Series, 04-05, College of Business Administration, Northern Arizona University, 2004.

[31] Joseph, Veroff, Elizebeth, Douvan, and Richard A. Kulka, *The inner American: A self-portrait from 1957–1976* (New York: basic Books, 1981).

[32] Richard A. Easterlin, 'Does Economic Growth Improve the Human Lot? Some Empirical Evidence', in, PA David & MW Reder (eds) *Nations and Households in Economic Growth: Essays in Honor of Moses Abramowitz,* (1974)Academic Press,

[33] John Knight and Ramani Gunatilaka, 'The Rural-Urban Divide in China', 506–534.

5   Results

Factors associated with subjective well-being

Table 15.1 (refer annexure) presents the results of estimating the happiness functions of married employed women and married homemakers using OLS. Factors associated with happiness are examined under the main roles which married women play, along with demographic controls and the economic and household controls. Model 1 contains the family-related variables, along with the variables relevant to the roles of daughter and daughter-in-law. Model 2 introduces the variables related to the role of a wife, and model 3 introduces the variables related to the role of mother. Her role as an income earner is introduced in model 4; model 5 shows the full equation which has family role-related variables, employment role-related variable, demographic, economic and household control variables.

Housework made married women unhappy and being primarily responsible for housework added on to the unhappiness. Being appreciated by family members had a significantly positive impact on happiness. The ability to achieve childhood goals was significantly important in increasing happiness until resources required for goal achievement such as income and level education were controlled for. Recent bereavements made married women unhappy and significantly so when income and demographics were controlled for.

When it came to the role of a daughter, the relationship with own parents added on to happiness but not significantly, whereas the relationship with in-laws, was important for a married women's happiness only before controlling for the role of a wife and motherhood related variables. On the other hand, having your own mother reside close to your own house was negatively related to a married woman's happiness.

Considering the role of a wife, a close relationship with the husband had a very powerful significant impact on happiness. Although the value of the coefficient of this variable was marginally dropped with the introduction of motherhood, employment, demographic and income related variables, the strong significance remained even in the last equation, illustrating the importance of the relationship with husband in determining the wife's level of happiness. Husband not being very supportive in sharing household duties reduced happiness but not significantly so in any of the equations.

Next we considered variables related to the role of a mother. Having children below 5 years old had a significantly positive correlation until employment was controlled for, whereas having children between the ages of 5–11, made married women unhappy throughout all three equations. Children between the ages of 12–16 seemed to generally make mother's happy, but the coefficient emerged as significant only when demographic and income variables were controlled. Extent to which the respondent is satisfied with her children's welfare had a very strong positive impact on happiness before demographic and income related variables were included. Our overall results related to the role of a mother seemed to be in line with international research where motherhood is known to make life wonderful as well as miserable[34].

Being employed – or currently being involved in an income earning activity – had a very strong negative correlation with a married woman's reported level of happiness. The negative significance remained even after controlling for demographic and income related variables. The value of the employment coefficient was considerably large compared to majority of other variables. This enabled us to answer one of our key research questions, who is happier? The employed wife or the homemaker? With these results we see that being engaged in market work significantly decreases the married woman's subjective well-being, compared with those who do not engage in market work.

Then we looked at demographic related variables. Age (negative) and age squared (positive) both did not have a significant impact on happiness. When ethnicity and religion were considered, none of the ethno-religious dummies were significant in influencing married women's happiness, but Sinhalese Christian women were happier than the Tamil Christian, Tamil Hindu and Islamic moor women. None of the education related variables turned out to have a significant correlation with happiness, although a monotonic increase in the coefficients from one education level to the next could be seen up to the Advanced Level. Being in good health raised married women's happiness.

Next we considered income related variables. Log of household per capita income had a significantly positive correlation with happiness when it was used as the only income related variable. However when relative income related variables were introduced the significance was gradually reduced. Subjective opinions about monthly income and expenses also had a significant positive impact on happiness. Being in debt reduced a married woman's happiness, although not significantly. Both temporal income comparison variables had a significant impact on happiness, where an improvement of the living standards compared to 5 years ago raised happiness and a deterioration in living standards reduced happiness. Social comparisons seemed to be very important in determining a married woman's happiness. Considering oneself to be doing better than the reference category increased happiness, but considering that they are doing far worse than the reference category had the most detrimental impact on a married woman's happiness. Living in a house owned by

---

34   Barnett and Baruch, 'Women's Involvement in Multiple Roles'.

herself or by a family member had a significant positive impact on happiness and being satisfied about housing conditions also added on to happiness.

6 Conclusion

This paper mainly finds that going out to work, in addition to their other caregiving responsibilities, makes married working women's subjective well-being lower than homemakers. We also find that being happily married, well appreciated, having children who are doing well in life, being able to achieve childhood goals, and being able to easily manage monthly expenses, all seems to be having a positive impact on married women's happiness. However, women who feel that they are burdened with household duties, and women who consider their own living standards to be much lower than the reference category, seem to be relatively unhappy.

Bibliography

Alvarez, Begona and Daniel Miles. *Women's Subjective Well-Being and Housework Allocation*. Spain: Department of Applied Economics, University of Vigo, 2012.

Andre, Rae. *Homemakers: The Forgotten Workers*. Chicago: University of Chicago Press, 1981.

Barnett, Rosalind and Grace K. Baruch. 'Women's Involvement in Multiple Roles, Role Strain, and Psychological Distress'. *Journal of Personality and Social Psychology* 49(1985): 135–145.

Beja Jr, Edsel L. 'Who is Happier: House Wife or Working Wife?'. *Applied Research in Quality of Life* 9.2 (2014): 157–177.

Bender, Keith A, Susan M. Donohue, and John S. Heywood. 'Job satisfaction and gender segregation'. *Oxford Economic Papers* 57 (2005): 479–496.

Benin, Mary H. and Babara C. Nienstedt. 'Happiness in Single and Dual-Earner Families: The Effects of Marital Happiness, Job Satisfaction, and Life Cycle'. *Journal of Marriage and Family* 47.4 (1985): 975–984.

Berk, Richard A. and Sarah F. Berk. *Labor and Leisure at Home: Content and Organization of the Household Day*. California: Sage, 1979.

Berk, Sarah F. *The Gender Factory: The Apportionment of Work in American Households*. New York: Plenum, 1985.

Bird, Chloe E. and Catherine E. Ross. 'House Workers and Paid Workers: Qualities of the Work and Effects on Personal Control'. *Journal of Marriage and the Family* 55.9 (1993): 13–25.

Boye, Katarina. 'Work and Well-Being in a Comparative Perspective – The Role of Family Policy'. *European Sociological Review* 27.1 (2011): 16–30.

Campione, Wendy. 'Voluntary job change versus employer promotion: Do women fare better on their own?'. *Journal of Applied Business and Economics* 6 (2006): 14–28.

Campione, Wendy. 'Employed Women's Well-being: The Global and Daily Impact of Work'. *Journal of Family and Economics Issues* 29.3 (2008): 346.

Campione, Wendy, Morgan, James and Jerrell, Max 2004, 'Employed Women's Well-being: The Global and Daily Impact of Work', Working Paper Series,04-05, College of Business Administration, Northern Arizona University,2004.

Department of Census and Statistics, *Census of Population and Housing 2012*. Colombo: Ministry of Finance and Planning, 2012.

Department of Census and Statistics, *Sri Lanka Labour Force Survey Annual Report 2012*. Colombo: Ministry of Finance and Planning, 2012.

DeVault, Marjorie L. *Feeding the Family: The Social Organization of Caring as Gerldered Work.* Chicago: University of Chicago Press, 1991.

Easterlin. A. Richard. 'Does Economic Growth Improve the Human Lot? Some Empirical Evidence', in, PA David & MW Reder (eds) *Nations and Households in Economic Growth: Essays in Honor of Moses Abramowitz,* (1974)Academic Press, 89–125

Ferree, Myra M. 'Class, Housework, and Happiness: Women's Work and Life Satisfaction'. *Sex Roles* 1.1(1984): 1057–1074.

Freudiger, Patricia. 'Life Satisfaction Among Three Categories of Married Women'. *Journal of Marriage and Family*, 45.1 (1983): 213–219.

Goode, William J. 'A Theory of Strain'. *American Sociological Review* 25 (1960): 483–496.

Graham, Lowe S and Herbert C. Northcott. 'The Impact of Working Conditions, Social Roles, and Personal Characteristics on Gender Differences in Distress'. *Work and Occupations* 15 (1988): 55–77.

Gunasekera, Sirohmi. *Sri Lanka, Working Mothers and Baby Blues*. Viewed 11 September 2009. http://newsblaze.com/story/20090902063301iwfs.nb/topstory.html.

Gunatilaka, Ramani. 'To work or not to work? Factors Holding Women back from Market Work in Sri Lanka'. *ILO Asia-Pacific Working Paper Series*. New Delhi: DWT for South Asia and Country Office for India, 2013.

Hennig, Marina., Stefan Stuth, Mareike Ebach, and Anna E. Hägglund. 'How do Employed Women Perceive the Reconciliation of Work and Family Life?: A Seven-Country Comparison of the Impact of Family Policies on Women's Employment'. *International Journal of Sociology and Social Policy* 32.9 (2012): 513 – 529.

Hochschild, Arlie and Anne Machung. *The Second Shift: Working Parents and the Revolution at Home.* New York: Academic Press, 1989.

Hochschild, Arlie R. *The Time Bind: When Work Becomes Home and Home Becomes Work.* New York: Henry Holy, 1997.

Horley, James and John J. Lavery. 'Subjective Well-Being and Age'. *Social Indicators Research* 34 (1995): 275–282.

International Labour Organization (ILO). 'Globalization, Employment and Gender in the Open Economy of Sri Lanka', *Employment Working Paper Series* 138. Employment Sector: Employment Policy Department, 2013.

Kariyawasam, Sanjeewanie, Nilakshi De Silva and Shivapragasam Shivakumaran. 'Multi-Dimensional Poverty among Samurdhi Welfare Recipients in Badulla District Sri Lanka'. *PMMA Working Paper*, Centre for Poverty Analysis, Sri Lanka, Partnership for Economic Policy, 2012.

Knight, John and Ramani Gunatilaka. 'The Rural-Urban Divide in China: Income but not Happiness?'. *Journal of Developmental Studies* 46.3 (2010): 506–534.

Lee, Gary R., Karen Seccombe, and Constance L. Shehan. 'Marital Status and Personal Happiness: An Analysis of Trend Data'. *Journal of Marriage and the Family* 53 (1991): 839–844.

Lennon, Mary C. 'Women, Work and Well-Being: The Importance of Work Conditions'. *Journal of Health and Social Behaviour* 35 (1994): 235–247.

Luhmann, Maike, Hofmann, Wilhelm, Eid, Micheal and Lucas, Richard E. 'Subjective Well-Being and Adaptation to Life Events: A Meta-Analysis on Differences Between Cognitive and Affective Well-Being'. *Journal of Personality and Social Psychology*, 102.3 (2012): 592–615.

Lyubomirsky, Sonja., Chris Tkach, and Robin M. DiMatteo. 'What are the Differences between Happiness and Self-Esteem?'. *Social Indicators Research* 78 (2006): 363–404.

Malhotra, Anju and Deborah S. Degraff. 'Daughters and Wives: Marital Status, Poverty and Young Women's Employment in Sri Lanka'. *Women Poverty and Demographic Change*, edited by Brigida Garcia, 145–174. Oxford: Oxford University Press Inc, 2000.

Marks, Stephen R. 'Multiple Roles and Role Strain: Some Notes on Human Energy, Time and Commitment'. *American Sociological Review* 41 (1977): 921–936.

Michalos, Alex C. 'Multiple discrepancies theory (MDT)'. *Social indicators research* 16.4 (1985): 347–413.

Ministry of Labour Relations and Manpower, Central Bank of Sri Lanka, Department of Census and Statistics. 'Labour and Social Trends in Sri Lanka', *Recent Economic Labour Market and Social Developments* (2009): 6.

Oakley, Ann. *The Sociology of Housework*. New York: Pantheon, 1974.

Oswald, Andrew J. 'Happiness and Economic Performance'. *Economic Journal* 107.445(1997): 1815–1831.

Ott, Bryant. *More Sri Lankans Suffering since the War Ended*. Viewed 16 February 2013. http://www.gallup.com/poll/153779/Sri-Lankans-Suffering-War-Ended.aspx

Pearlin, Leonard I. 'Life-Span Developmental Psychology: Normative Life Crises'. *Sex Roles and Depression*, edited by Nancy Datan and Leon H. Ginsberg, 191–207. New York: Academic Press, 1975.

Pezzini, Silvia, 'The Effect of Women's Rights on Women's Welfare: Evidence from a Natural Experiment'. *The Economic Journal* 115 (2005): C208–C227.

Pleck, Joseph H. *Working Wives/Working Husbands.* California: Sage,1985.

Rajadhyaksha, Ujvala and Deepti Bhatnagar. 'Life Role Salience: A Study of Dual Career Couples in the Indian Context'. *Human Relations* 53 (2000): 489–511.

Rosenfield, Sarah. 'Sex Differences in Depression: Do Women Always Have Higher Rates?'. *Journal of Health and Social Behavior* 21 (1980): 33–42.

Samarasinghe, Gameela and Chandrika Ismail, *A Psychological Study of Blue Collar Female Workers*. Colombo -06: Women's Education and Research Centre, 2000.

Sanjeewanie Kariyawasam. 'Comparative Perspective: Gendered Dimensions of Well-Being'. Paper Presented at the 13th National Convention on Women's Studies, Centre for Women's Research Sri Lanka, July 27–30, 2012: 10.

Satharasinghe, Amara J. 'Time-Use Analysis of Husbands and Wives'. *Sri Lanka Journal of Population Studies* 2 (1999): 11–24.

Smith, Courtland and Patricia Clay. 'Measuring Subjective and Objective Well-Being: Analyses from Five Marine Commercial Fisheries'. *Human Organization* 69.2 (2010): 158–168.

Stock, William A., Morris A. Okun, Marilyn J. Haring, and Robert A. Witter. 'Age and Subjective Well-Being: A Meta Analysis'. *Evaluation Studies: Review Annual,* edited by R J Light, 279–302. California: Sage, 1983.

Stutzer, A and Frey, BS, 'Reported Subjective Well-being: A Challenge for Economic theory and Economic Policy', *Schmollers Jahrbuch,*,124(2004):191–231.

Stutzer, A 2004, 'The role of income aspirations in individual happiness', *Journal of Economic Behavior and Organization,* 54.1(2004)89–109.

United Nations Development Programme (UNDP) Sri Lanka. *Sri Lanka Human Development Report 2012: Bridging Regional Disparities for Human Development.* Colombo:UNDP Sri Lanka, 2012.

Veroff, Joseph, Elizebeth, Douvan, and Richard A. Kulka. *The inner American: A self-portrait from 1957–1976* (New York: basic Books, 1981).

Weerackody, Chaminda and Saman Fernando. *Reflections on Mental Health and Well-Being, Learning from Communities Affected by Conflict, Dislocation and Natural Disasters in Sri Lanka.* Colombo, People's Rural Development Association (PRADA), 2011.

Weerackody, Chaminda and Saman Fernando. *Mental Health and Well-Being, Experience of Communities Affected by Conflict, and 2004 Tsunami in Sri Lanka.* Colombo: People's Rural Development Association (PRADA) & Oxfam America, 2009.

Wilson Warner R. 'Correlates of Awowed Happiness'. *Psychological Bulletin* 67 (1967): 294–306.

Wright, James D. 'Are Working Women Really more Satisfied? Evidence from Several National Surveys'. *Journal of Marriage and Family.* 40.2 (1978): 301–313.

Annexure

TABLE 15.1 Regression Analysis

Role	Variable	Model 1	Model 2	Model 3	Model 4	Model 5
Family	Number of hours spent doing housework per day	-0.0498*** (0.0111)	-0.0500*** (0.0109)	-0.0472*** (0.0109)	-0.0574*** (0.0120)	-0.0368*** (0.0121)
	There is no one else to do housework	-0.4434*** (0.1180)	-0.3225*** (0.1171)	-0.2891** (0.1169)	-0.2698** (0.1172)	-0.2282** (0.1138)
	Extent to which she is being appreciated by family	0.2385*** (0.0410)	0.1522*** (0.0424)	0.1255*** (0.0426)	0.1315*** (0.0426)	0.0782* (0.0419)
	Extent to which childhood goals have been achieved	0.0588*** (0.0226)	0.0540** (0.0221)	0.0507** (0.0219)	0.0604*** (0.0225)	0.0256 (0.0228)
	Death of a close family member – last 5 years	-0.0996 (0.0694)	-0.0879 (0.0679)	-0.0927 (0.0673)	-0.0949 (0.0672)	-0.1498** (0.0650)
Daughter	Extent to which the respondent is satisfied about relationship with parents	0.0237 (0.0308)	0.0152 (0.0302)	0.0162 (0.0303)	0.0164 (0.0302)	0.0296 (0.0307)
	Mother is residing close by to own house	-0.1027 (0.0767)	-0.1395* (0.0753)	-0.1421* (0.0748)	-0.1395* (0.0747)	-0.1284* (0.0731)
Daughter-in-law	Extent to which the respondent is satisfied about relationship with in laws	0.0543* (0.0277)	0.0247 (0.0275)	0.0169 (0.0274)	0.0156 (0.0274)	-0.0095 (0.0264)
Wife	Extent to which relationship with husband can be described as close		0.2457*** (0.0430)	0.2217*** (0.0435)	0.2172*** (0.0435)	0.1391*** (0.0431)
	Husband is not supportive with housework		-0.0607	-0.0553	-0.0598	-0.0500

Mother	Total number of children in the HH – below 5 yrs.	(0.0585)	(0.0581) 0.0839* (0.0471)	(0.0580) 0.0713 (0.0475)	(0.0559) 0.0352 (0.0536)
	Total number of children in the HH – between 5 and 11		-0.0452 (0.0388)	-0.0524 (0.0389)	-0.0658 (0.0425)
	Total number of children in the HH – between 12 and 16		0.0396 (0.0463)	0.0451 (0.0463)	0.0834* (0.0494)
	Extent to which the respondent is satisfied with her children's welfare		0.1478*** (0.0387)	0.1515*** (0.0387)	0.0688* (0.0391)
Employed	Currently employed			-0.1199* (0.0619)	-0.1384** (0.0626)
Demographic Controls	Age				-0.0284 (0.0266)
	Age squared				0.0003 (0.0003)
	Sinhala Christian				0.0910 (0.1042)
	Tamil Hindu				-0.0098 (0.0788)

TABLE 15.1 (cont.)

Role	Variable	Model 1	Model 2	Model 3	Model 4	Model 5
	Tamil Christian					-0.0131
						(0.2122)
	Islamic Moor					-0.1161
						(0.0761)
	Secondary education					0.0067
						(0.1375)
	Ordinary Level					0.1492
						(0.1388)
	Advanced Level					0.1881
						(0.1425)
	Degree					0.1730
						(0.1689)
	In good health					0.1140
						(0.1023)
Economic and household controls	Log of per capita HH income					0.4805
						(0.6522)
	Log of per capita HH income squared					-0.0208
						(0.0342)
	Currently in debt					-0.0954
						(0.0607)

Agreement to "Can easily manage monthly income and expenses"	0.0955** (0.0374)
Current living standard better than 5 years ago	0.1287* (0.0705)
Current living standard worse than 5 years ago	-0.2309* (0.1246)
Household living standards are higher than the reference group	0.1994 (0.1228)
Household living standards are same as the reference group	0.1056 (0.0647)
Household living standards are below the reference group	0.0027 (0.0745)
Household living standards are much below than the reference group	-0.2763** (0.1084)
Satisfaction with house	0.0568 (0.0371)
Living in own or family owned house	0.1442* (0.0792)

TABLE 15.1 (cont.)

Role Variable	Model 1	Model 2	Model 3	Model 4	Model 5
Constant	2.9444***	2.3258***	1.8203***	1.8894***	0.0092
	(0.2003)	(0.2454)	(0.2783)	(0.2801)	(3.1713)
R-squared	0.1100	0.1510	0.1710	0.1750	0.2760
N	838	838	838	838	838

Notes:
1. Dependent variables: score of happiness is based on cardinal values assigned to qualitative assessments as follows: very happy = 5; happy = 4; so-so =3; not happy = 2 and not at all happy =1.
2. Independent variables with cardinal values assigned to qualitative assessments so that greater intensity is represented by a higher value are: extent to which she is appreciated by family, extent to which childhood goals have been achieved, extent to which the respondent is satisfied about relationship with parents, extent to which the respondent is satisfied about relationship with in laws, extent to which relationship with husband can be described as close, extent to which the respondent is satisfied with her children's welfare, agreement to the statement "can easily manage monthly income and expenses", satisfaction with house.
3. The omitted categories in the dummy variable analyses are: Sinhala-Buddhist, primary educated, not healthy, no death in the family – last 5 yrs, husband is supportive with housework, currently not employed, others help with housework, mother does not live close by, currently not in debt, current living standard is same as 5 years ago, do not make social comparisons, not living in own or family owned house.
4. The standard errors are shown in brackets underneath
5. In this table, ***, **, and * denote statistical significance at the 1 per cent, 5 per cent and 10 per cent levels, respectively.

CHAPTER 16

The Sublime Landscape

Jane Russell-O'Connor

Abstract

The experience of landscape can make us happy. Landscape has been a topic of interest for hundreds of years, but discussion has been largely concerned with the aesthetic values of a landscape where it has been viewed *as the eye sees it* and painted or drawn. The term was used by Dutch painters in the 16th century to describe the countryside in terms of the scenery that was painted.[1] However landscape is often associated with the sublime, when considering the transcending of beauty, as the experience of emotions one feels when standing in a beautiful place observing a magnificent vista. It is more than the beauty of the landscape, but the culmination of a number of factors such as the physical, emotional and spiritual elements of landscape, that lead to these happy feelings. The sublime may not always be considered in a tranquil landscape but also in the dramatic, exciting and dangerous landscape. For example, in the 17th and 18th centuries such contrasts were observed by Dennis (1688), Cooper (1709), and Addison (1712) when they each trekked through the Alps and related the sublime to the horrors and the harmony of the experiences of being in such a landscape.[2] This paper aims to explore the sublime landscape and how it relates to human happiness. I set out to capture, as discussed by Appleton,[3] where the aesthetics of landscape are related to peoples' feelings and perceptions by answering such questions as 'What is it we like about landscape and why do we like it?' Such questions allow us to ponder not only the beauty of a landscape and why it is so, but furthermore the stimulation of our other senses and the sense of the sublime achieved. The experience of the sublime is arguably part of a flourishing life.

Keywords

landscape – sublime – aesthetic – biophilia – seascapes – delightful horrors

---

1 John Barrell, *The Idea of Landscape and the Sense of Place 1730–1840* (Cambridge: Cambridge University Press, 1972).
2 Simon Schama, *Landscape and Memory* (London: Fontana Press, 1996).
3 Jay Appleton, *The Experience of Landscape* (Chichester: Wiley and Sons, 1975).

1 Introduction

The happiness experienced in landscape can be related to the joy of discovery and how landscapes are dynamic and constantly changing. Whether it be the dappled light through the soft, delicate, bright green leaves slowly unfurling in a canopy above the violet flowers of bluebells carpeting the undergrowth, coupled with the freshness of spring in the air and the musical song of birds singing joyously at the new, emerging life. Or in the same woodland, the stark contrast of the dark, bare branches of the trees against the backdrop of blinding white snow glinting in the pale sunlight of a winter' day, the bark of a fox in the distance and the soft sound of footfall on the blanketed ground. This exploration of the new, as well as the dangerous, will be discussed, both of which feed our primal instinct and can give rise to happiness.

2 Landscape Research

Although landscape has been a topic of interest for many hundreds of years from largely an aesthetic point of view, where landscape was immortalised in paintings, the more scholarly approach to landscape has been developed into two well established disciplines of research: landscape ecology and landscape history. Landscape ecology is interdisciplinary research that has a more positivist approach focusing on the ecological understanding of spatial heterogeneity. This discipline covers applied research into the relationships between the biophysical components of landscape as well as the socioeconomic influences, the management, conservation and sustainability of landscape. Landscape history, which has a more interpretative approach, concerns itself with the ways in which humans have changed the landscape and deals with the cultural aspects of landscape. Landscape ecology, whilst wide ranging and important, especially in conserving the diversity of species, habitats and *naturalness* of landscapes, does not consider the emotional attachment we humans have with the landscape. Landscape history does however consider the human attachment with the landscape, but usually in terms culture such as the way in which landscape has been recorded in, for example, maps, travel journals, estate records, and creative interpretation in poetry or music and so on.

However, neither of these disciplines explores our intense emotional relationship with the landscape, which harks back to our animal origins, where an appreciation of the landscape was crucial to human survival. This is the essence of the *biophilia hypothesis* which was defined by Edward Wilson in the early 1980s, as the instinct of staying alive.[4] As humans we have spent over three million years in nature and as thus have developed an innate connection with the natural landscape. The phenomenon of biophilia has spanned many different cultures and further research has determined that our preference for certain aspects of nature are universal. For example, landscapes with trees, vistas, water and a rich variety of plants.[5] In terms of biophilia these preferences are related to the fear associated with predators in that open vistas allow us to see approaching predators, trees allow us to hide and so on.[6] Although biophilia concerns itself with the fear of predators and instinct for self-preservation it highlights our emotional connection with nature and in particular landscape.

If we today undertake a journey up a mountain or along a river is there not a need to explore what is over the next peak or round the next bend? This sense of exploration, of delight in the landscape that often causes us to stop and take in the vistas from the mountain-view or the fast flowing water of the river and the luscious vegetation along its banks, is much more than the appreciation of the aesthetic beauty. It gives rise to an emotional response whereby there is a sense of peace, a sense of belonging, a sense of contentment. This again relates back to our early ancestors and our primal instincts where these types of landscapes were essential for survival such as the river for food and water and the mountains providing an advantage point from which to view oncoming predators. This view is also held by Dutton, who writes about similar experiences when one is travelling along an unknown country road, taking pleasure from the views and the vegetation and likens the travel along the road to that of travelling along a river by our ancestors and in doing so captures remnants of our past.[7]

3   Delightful Horrors

Conventionally beautiful landscapes were considered at the opposite end of the emotional spectrum compared with landscapes that inspire reverence,

---

4   Edward O. Wilson, *Biophilia* (Cambridge: Harvard University Press, 1984).
5   Eva Selhub and Alan Logan, *Your Brain on Nature: The Science of Natures Influence on your Health Happiness and Vitality* (Ontario: Wiley and Sons, 2012).
6   Ibid.
7   Dennis Dutton, *The art instinct: beauty, pleasure, & human evolution*, (Oxford: Oxford University Press, 2009).

horror or fear (that is, the sublime).[8] John Dennis who crossed the Alps in 1688 thought he had:

> walked upon the very brink in a litteral sense, of Destruction; one stumble, and both Life and Carcass had at once both been destroy'd. The sense of all of this produc'd different emotions in me, viz. delightful Horrour, a terrible Joy and at the same time that I was infinitely pleas'd, I trembled.[9]

Thomas Gray and Horace Walpole, who in 1739 embarked on a journey of experimental sensation, across the Alps, toyed with disaster and took delight in the dangerous and the terror experienced by earlier explorers like John Dennis (1688) Anthony Ashley Cooper (1709), and Joseph Addison (1712).[10]

In contrast to the delightful horrors of those 17th and 18th century explorers of the Alps, the modern day definition of the sublime appears somewhat different. For example, the Oxford English definition for sublime as: 'Producing an overwhelming sense of awe or other high emotion through being vast or grand'.[11] This definition is one that is more commonly understood today when one thinks of the sublime. Despite the differences in the meaning of the word used in the 17th and 18th centuries compared with more modern times, it still evokes an emotional response when concerned with the landscape. In contrast the term *beautiful landscape* perhaps today conjures one of tranquillity, such as a hot sunny day with gently lapping waves on a golden beach, or delicate flowers and ruminating cows on an undulating alpine meadow, or a babbling brook flowing through the woodland. All of these allow us to feel calm, peaceful and contented. In stark contrast to these are the drama of the violent white waves crashing against the rocks blackened by the darkened sky above and the continual battering of the water, the majestic snowy mountains where there is a stillness and quietness, unlike anywhere else. Such scenes evoke a wonder, a reverence of the sublime landscape on view. All of these different landscapes are filled with life and an energy force that is transferred to humans which give rise to happiness and joy.

---

8   Paul Selman and Carys Swanick, 'On the Meaning of Natural Beauty in Landscape Legislation', *Landscape Research* 35:1(2010): 3–26.
9   John Dennis, *Miscellanies in Prose and Verse*, (London: Printed for James Knapton by The Crown in St Pauls Church Yard, 1692), 134.
10 Schama, *Landscape and Memory*.
11 OED, *Oxford Dictionaries*, (Oxford: Oxford University Press, 2016), viewed 4 February 2016, http://www.oxforddictionaries.com/definition/english/sublime.

4   Healing Landscape

The concept of the natural environment as a mental healer is not new and gained popularity in the late 19th century where the writer Henry David Thoreau and naturalist John Muir wrote about nature being essential to well-being.

Muir wrote 'tired, nerve shaken, over civilised people could experience awakening while wandering in wilderness'.[12] A view also supported by Ulrich et al., who found that signs of stress were reduced in people when they looked at landscapes with trees, lakes or meadows.[13] There are reoccurring themes that relate beautiful landscape to improved mental health. The sheer number of activities that are undertaken in the wilderness or in the landscape are testament to this. Furthermore, it is not only the act of seeing and being in a landscape can make one feel better, but also the doing – physical activity in the landscape that can improve our state of mind. However the climbing of a mountain is not just about the physical exertion involved in getting to the top, or the conquering of nature, or the getting away from it all, it is the spiritual element of connectedness with the landscape. We climb to see what is up there, to experience that sense of space, to take in the vistas, to be awed by the vastness and the danger. The experience as a whole makes us feel better and can lead to happiness.

5   Perceptions of Landscape

To explore different perceptions of landscape, research was conducted with a number of undergraduate architecture students at Waterford Institute of Technology in Ireland. Out of the 78 students questioned about what elements of the landscape they found to be aesthetically pleasing, only 35% included buildings in a visually pleasing landscape, of which a mere 8% were modern buildings. When asked why buildings did not feature more in their beautiful landscapes, the majority of these trainee architects considered natural landscapes more visually pleasing. Vegetation, water and mountains ranked highly as the most important components of aesthetically pleasing landscapes. When asked about the motivations for visiting these landscapes, the students replied 'that they were places to escape to', place to think and ultimately places where

---

12   John Muir, *Our National Parks* (Austin: Houghton, Mifflin and Company, 1901), 1.
13   Roger S. Ulrich, et al., 'Stress recovery during exposure to natural and urban environments', *Journal of Environmental Psychology*, 20.4, (1991): 355–373.

they found happiness.[14] This research has been repeated over the last few years and the results have been replicated, with now over 400 students being questioned, whereby the responses are similar. It does seem to appear that happiness in the landscape relates to landscapes that are open, with appealing vegetation, water and often mountains, which relates back to the biophilia theory. When asked about people in the landscape, the majority of students stated that, apart from the people they were with (and sometimes no-one) people were absent in the landscape. Dutton similarly researched peoples' perceptions of beautiful landscapes and found that their desirability increased significantly in landscapes involving water.[15]

Nichols explored, from a neuroscience perspective, how humans' connection with water can result in calmness, improved performance, improved health and, amongst other things, happiness. I would certainly support this from my own experience as a wild swimmer in the Celtic sea off the coast of Waterford in Ireland.[16]

My swimming friends and I exit our cars on a cool autumn morning, breathe in the sea air, look out across the wide expanse of Tramore bay and descend the many steps to the Guillamine swimming cove. We take off our clothes down to our swimsuits as quickly as possible in the cold air, don our swimming caps and head off down to the water's edge. With a deep breath we then launch ourselves into the cold sea one by one, each shivering, and sometimes yelping with surprise at the coldness, as we swim away. After a few seconds, the icy chill elicits a gasp and is replaced by a warm tingle as we swim out towards some pre-arranged point. I feel a connection with the sea, the sky, and the birds on the rocks. I take in the colours as I swim: the brown seaweed wracks floating in the waves attached to nearby rocks, the yellow green and white lichen clinging to the rocks of the cliffs around us, the blue sky above, the black sea below, teaming with life that I do not really want to think about too much, especially the life that is bigger than me. As we three exit from the sea, our skin is tinged pink with the coldness of the water but we are no longer cold, merely refreshed, awakened and alive. The feeling of exhilaration, euphoria and happiness is immense. I have never left the sea and felt anything other than these

---

14   Jane Russell-O'Connor 'Student Perceptions of Landscape: Developing a Methodology of Landscape Assessment for Architects' (Paper presented at the Annual Irish Architecture Research Group Conference University of Limerick, Ireland, January 25–26, 2013).
15   Dutton, *The art instinct: beauty, pleasure, & human evolution.*
16   Wallace J. Nichols, *Blue Mind: The surprising science that shows how being near in, on or under water can make you happier, healthier, more connected and better at what you do* (New York: Little Brown, 2014).

emotions. To me this multifaceted, multisensory landscape, is and will always be a place I hold in awe, a sublime landscape; a happy place to be.

Bibliography

Appleton, Jay. *The Experience of Landscape*. Chichester: Wiley and Sons, 1975.

Barrell, John. *The Idea of Landscape and the Sense of Place 1730–1840*. Cambridge: Cambridge University Press, 1972.

Dennis, John. *Miscellanies in Prose and Verse*, London: Printed for James Knapton by The Crown in St Pauls Church Yard, 1692.

Dutton, Denis. *The art instinct: beauty, pleasure, & human evolution*. Oxford: Oxford University Press, 2009.

Muir, John. *Our National Parks*. Austin: Houghton, Mifflin and Company, 1901.

Nichols, Wallace J. *Blue Mind: The surprising science that shows how being near in, on or under water can make you happier, healthier, more connected and better at what you do*. New York: Little Brown, 2014.

OED. *Oxford Dictionaries*. Oxford: Oxford University Press, 2016. Viewed 4 February 2016, http://www.oxforddictionaries.com/definition/english/sublime.

Russell-O'Connor, Jane. 'Student Perceptions of Landscape: Developing a Methodology of Landscape Assessment for Architects'. Paper presented at the Annual Irish Architecture Research Group Conference, University of Limerick, Ireland, January 25–26, 2013.

Schama, Simon. *Landscape and Memory*. London: Fontana Press, 1996.

Selhub, Eva. and Alan Logan. *Your Brain on Nature: The Science of Natures Influence on your Health Happiness and Vitality*. Ontario: Wiley and Sons, 2012.

Selman, Paul. and Carys Swanick. 'On the Meaning of Natural Beauty in Landscape Legislation', *Landscape Research* 35:1(2010): 3–26.

Ulrich, Robert S., Robert F. Simmons, Barbara D. Losito, Evelyn R. Fiorito, Mark A. Miles and Michael Zelson. 'Stress recovery during exposure to natural and urban environments', *Journal of Environmental Psychology*, 20.4, (1991): 355–373.

Wilson, Edward O. *Biophilia*. Cambridge: Harvard University Press, 1984.

Index

aboriginal art   64, 66–67
active vocation   76
aponia   129, 132, 134
aquinas's development of Aristotle's theory   112–113
Aristotelian hexis   11
Aristotle's concept   14–19
Aristotle's theory, aquinas's development of   112–113
art therapy techniques   50–61

Bateson, Gregory   122, 122n24
Beaumont, Marie Le Prince de   41, 41n1
beauty and the beast   41–48
biophilia hypothesis   160–161

Chuang Tzu   104n21, 105
classic cars   80–86
completeness   15, 99
consent   44, 48
contemporary domestic lifestyles   52
course topics   66–67
creative and influential home   51
Csikszentmihalyi, Mihalyi   50, 51n1, 52n11, 60n28, 73, 73n4, 74n6
cultural ecology   121–122

day reconstruction method (DRM)   29–38
delightful horrors   161–162
Dennis, John   159, 161n7, 162, 162n9
De Rurum Natura   135
dialectical abstraction   45–46
DRM *See* day reconstruction method (DRM)
duplex thesis   111

earthly happiness   108–115
emptiness   98–106
eudaimonia   14–19
experiential holism   90–92

facilitating emotional expression   50, 59–60
fairy tales   42, 45
feeling good   14–19
finality   15
flesh-pots   136
folk-healing   130
Ford Clubs   85

freedom of association   23
fullness   98–106

Gibbs, Paul   7, 7n2, 10, 10n11
good life, overview of   64–70
Gramsci, Antonio   42, 44–45
Gray, Thomas   162
gross imprudence   23

Haybron, Daniel   88n1, 89n6, 120n19
healing landscape   163
heavenly happiness   108–115
hectic routine   7, 11
hedonism   88, 89, 90, 96, 111, 131, 131n11, 134
hegemonic systems
    controls, ideology and concept of happiness   46–48
    incomplete abstraction   44–46
    virtue of beauty   42–44
hegemony, theory of   44–45
Heidegger, Martin   8, 8n5, 9
higher education   5, 32, 67, 69, 117–126
higher pleasure   21
Hotz, Julia   11
human flourishing   14, 15, 23

ill-regulated desires   23
income   29, 31, 142, 147, 148
    household   35, 36, 37–38
    scale   36
incomplete abstraction   42, 44–46
individual liberty   20, 23, 26
inferior pleasures   21
intellectual pleasure   92

Jefferson, Thomas   99, 100, 135–136

Kahneman, Daniel   29, 30n6, 31, 31n10, 33, 33n14, 89, 89n7, 137, 137n41
Kreider, Tim   136–137
Krueger, Anne   29, 31, 31n10
Kupperman, Joel   65, 65n1

landscape
    perceptions of   163–165
    research   160–161
Layard, Richard   109, 109n4, 110, 117n1

Lennon, Mary Clare 143, 143n11
liberty
    concept of 25
    of tastes and pursuits 23
life and times of epicurus 129–130
life trajectories 92–94
lower pleasure 21

Ma concept 103–105
Marx, Karl 41, 45, 46n11
mental healer 163
Mill, John Stuart 20n1, 23n14
moment-based hedonism 96
Muir, John 163, 163n12

Nakamura, Jeanne 50–51, 51n1
Nicomachean ethics 15, 15n3, 16, 110
Nussbaum, Martha 31, 32n13

objective wellbeing 110–112
ontological attitude of philosophers 8
open region 7, 10

Paleolithic lifestyle movement 138
participant interviews and survey 82–83
participant observation approach 54
Picard, Max 106
pleasure 18
    higher 21
    inferior 21
    intellectual 92
    lower 21
    sensual 136
positive family time 53–57, 60–61
preference-satisfaction theory 96

reaffirming natural imagery 23
reflective art making 50, 56–58
return of true epicurean happiness 136–138
routine of everyday life
    ontological sense of 8–10
    room is A-topos 10–12
Rybczynski, Zbigniew 9, 9n9

sacrilization 101–102
satisfaction
    job 123
    life 2, 5, 9, 29, 31–38, 88, 94, 140
    personal 3, 79

Schulz, Charles 99
secularization 101–102
self-sufficiency 15, 133, 136, 138
sensual pleasure 136
sexual gratification 136
Shinto shrine 102
silence art 53
Slow Food movement 137–138
spontaneous art 53
stability of State 27
Steward, Julian 121
student happiness expectations 67–69
subjective wellbeing (SWB) 109–110
    of married women 140–150
sublime landscape 159–165
SWB See subjective wellbeing (SWB)

themes 83–85
theory of hegemony 44–45
transcendence 7–13
Travolta, John 112

U- index 29
    activities by gender and 36
    activities by household income and 37
    correlations between 34
    ranking of activities by 35
unattractive dualism 95
utilitarianism 20

value of recreation 80–82
vicissitudes of fortune 23
virtue of beauty 42–44
virtuous life 17–18, 108
virtuous woman 111
visual anthropology 124–125
vocation fulfilment 72–78

Wallace, David Foster 68
Walpole, Horace 162
Waterman, Alan 34, 34n15
Weber, Max 73
wellbeing holism, forms of 90–92
Wilson, Edward 160
World Happiness Report 109, 117, 118
World Values Survey 30
Wu-wei 105

Zipes, Jack 42, 42n2, 43n4

Printed in the United States
By Bookmasters